"Consider this your survival guide on the sometimes rocky road to becoming a man. You're going to love this book!"

—Dr. Les Parrott,
author of *The Parent You Want to Be*

"*The Manual to Manhood* is an engaging, fun, and insightful how-to guide for guys on how to become a man. For those who want to build self-confidence, become independent, and fulfill your full potential, this book is for you."

—Sean Covey,
author of the international bestseller
The 7 Habits of Highly Effective Teens

"Every guy needs to know how to do everything in *The Manual to Manhood*. Jonathan is offering 'young men in the making' the truth about commonsense, real-world ways to gain respect and avoid embarrassment on the challenging road to manhood. Every young man should read this book!"

—Rick Johnson,
bestselling author of *Better Dads, Stronger Sons*
and *A Man in the Making: Strategies to Help
Your Son Succeed in Life*

"*The Manual to Manhood* is the perfect book for parents, teachers, coaches, and mentors looking to help boys learn valuable life lessons, develop strengths, and discover their unique identity on the journey to manhood."

—Matthew Ohlson, PhD,
College of Education, University of Florida,
education and school improvement consultant,
and proud father of three sons

THE
MANUAL TO
MANHOOD

How to
COOK the Perfect Steak,
CHANGE a Tire, IMPRESS a Girl
& 97 Other SKILLS You Need
to Survive

JONATHAN CATHERMAN

Revell

a division of Baker Publishing Group
Grand Rapids, Michigan

© 2014 by Jonathan Catherman

Published by Revell
a division of Baker Publishing Group
P.O. Box 6287, Grand Rapids, MI 49516-6287
www.revellbooks.com

Printed in the United States of America

Library of Congress Cataloging-in-Publication Data is on file at the Library of Congress, Washington, DC.

ISBN 978-0-8007-2229-6 (pbk.)

16 17 18 19 20 21 22   14 13 12 11 10 9 8

This book is dedicated to my sons,

Reed CatherMAN
and
Cole CatherMAN.

*Two strong, brave, and
courageous men in the making.*

Contents

Introduction

Welcome to manhood. Well ... almost. This "coming-of-age" stage in your life is guaranteed to introduce many highly anticipated opportunities you've been looking forward to. And much of what you are about to experience will put your manhood to the test—daily.

Speaking man-to-man, I can tell you that every guy wants the same two things. Do you know what they are? Before you laugh and say women and food, try thinking a bit differently. Here's the deal. At his core every man wants to gain respect and avoid embarrassment. The best of men know how to do both. And yes, learning to do each will benefit you, your relationships, and your BBQ skills.

Only you know how you got your hands on this manual. Maybe your mom gave it to you hoping it would teach you how to start shaving, grilling, or dating. Or maybe you picked it up yourself to avoid having your mom try to teach you to shave, show you how to grill, or put you through the embarrassment of her introducing you to a girl she thinks is "perfect" for you. Whatever the reason, remember this. Becoming a man requires practice—and despite what some people say, practice doesn't make perfect. Practice does make better, and you will become a better man for practicing what is captured on the pages of this *Manual to Manhood*.

First things first: take what you read in this book like a man. Start by not assuming you already know how to do everything. World-class experts were consulted about the best ways to do this stuff, and they were quick to admit that their way works but may not be the only way. You may know a different way to light a charcoal grill or iron a shirt. Good. Every man needs to develop his own style. No matter what your level of independence is, everybody needs to practice the life skills in this book—and for many readers, this will be an introduction to what every guy should learn and master.

Second, remember that performing the tasks of life with confidence and humility is done best when paired with a mature character. The top-shelf men consulted for this book recognize that becoming a man has little to do with age, size of muscles, or if a dude can grow a mustache or not. The world is populated by lots of guys with "manly" hairy chests who still act like immature boys. You have to earn the transformation from boyhood to manhood. And in doing so, you mature and secure without a doubt your title of "Man." There is no room for entitlement or false claims of maturity in the character of an authentic man. You have to work for it.

How a boy earns his manhood has changed over time and varies by location. Way back in the day, young Vikings joined their fathers in raiding parties. If a boy survived the raid, plundered the enemy, and shed blood, he proved himself and was from then on considered a man. On the South Pacific Island of Vanuatu, boys today still climb 100 feet up a tower, tie vines to their ankles, and dive headfirst bungee-style toward the ground. If a boy's leap is timed and measured correctly, he won't hit the dirt and his tribe will call him a man. In the "modern civilized" world, many guys act like chugging beast-sized power drinks, eating processed meat sticks, and killing each other virtually online is the magic formula needed to win their manliness. They are wrong.

Real men live by different standards, higher standards. Real men don't believe that the kind of car they drive, how much they drink, or the number of girls they get are what make them a man. Real men know that personal maturity transforms boys into men. Maturity is a practiced skill and is best demonstrated when a man knows how to do the right thing, the right way, at the right time, for the right reason. Even when nobody is looking. Are you this kind of man? You can be.

Your coming-of-age starts with a call to practice and master the solid life skills and mature character possessed by only the best of men. Consider this book your invitation . . .

WOMEN & DATING

1

Women. We men discover few things in the world that capture our attention quite like women. With so many men having the same focus, it's a good thing that about 50% of the planet's population is female. That means the odds are pretty good that you will run into a few ladies along the way who captivate you at levels you will find difficult to understand, let alone explain.

Though men and women share 99.7% of the same genes, it's the other 0.3% that makes the difference between our genders such a great mystery. Add to this intrigue the mix of emotions, hormones, and the coded way some girls talk, and it's no wonder most guys feel totally confused about how to interact successfully with women. One minute it feels impossible to live with them and the next it's impossible to live without them. You can't stop thinking about her yet you have no idea what she is thinking! What's a guy supposed to do?

According to Dr. Les Parrott, who just so happens to be one of the world's leading relationship experts, there is a three-part process every man needs to practice if he wants to better understand how to be in a good relationship with a woman.

1. **Be self-aware.** "If you want to have healthy relationships with anyone, especially women, you need to bring health to the relationship. Are you the best man you can be physically, emotionally, socially, and spiritually?" asks Dr. Parrott. "Your relationships can only be as healthy as you are. This means you must first be aware of your own emotions, needs, and goals in life."[1]

2. **Be aware of her.** "The most important thing you can do to build a healthy relationship is practice the skill of empathy. Empathy is key to a strong relationship because it is the act of setting aside your own selfish agenda to consider her needs. What are her feelings, thoughts, or attitude? What are her hopes and dreams? What are her concerns and fears? What are her goals in life?" Dr. Parrott goes on, "Empathy is not an easy skill to master because the way men's and women's brains think is so different. Our heads are hardwired in ways that lead us to naturally think and act differently.

Correctly imagining her perspective will take time and practice, but the results include greater levels of trust and understanding. This strengthens the relationship, which makes practicing empathy well worth the effort."

3. **Bring the two together.** To emphasize the point, Dr. Parrott instructs, "Men who can connect their self-awareness with a skill of empathy possess the twin engines and maturity needed to drive strong, healthy relationships."

Dr. Parrott is right. Guys can find a way to better understand and interact with women. Good thing too. Men and women were created to be perfect partners and lifelong companions. Learn what you can, yet keep in mind, not everything in life is meant to be understood. Some things are best valued when they retain a healthy level of mystery. Women included.

Meet Les Parrott III, PhD

Dr. Parrott is a #1 *New York Times* bestselling author and psychologist. Along with his wife, Leslie, he's authored books on love and marriage, selling more than 2 million copies in 30 different languages. An expert in relationship development, Dr. Parrott's groundbreaking work dedicated to teaching the basics of good relationships has led him to speak before hundreds of thousands of people around the world.

Talk with a Girl You Like

What would men be without women?
Scarce, sir ... mighty scarce.

—Mark Twain

YOU WILL NEED:

- A girl you like
- Courage
- Fresh breath
  (see "How to Freshen Bad Breath")

TIME REQUIRED:

- It will take as long as it takes.

There she is. This is your chance. Go over and say something! If you don't, some other guy will. He who hesitates loses and you're not a loser. So don't hesitate. You can talk to that girl, and here is how you're going to do it.

STEP 1 **Breathe.**

Before you take a step in her direction, take control of your breathing. You need breath to make words, so be sure to breathe normally. Hyperventilate and you'll talk too fast and get a brain buzz. Forget to breathe and you'll run out of the air needed to speak. The last thing you want is to lose your words before the end of your opening sentence.

STEP 2 **Check your breath.**

First impressions are important and you want this one to be fresh in her mind for a long time.

STEP 3 **Approach her with confidence.**

Stand tall with your shoulders back and your head held high. No slouching.

STEP 4 **Say something nice.**

Start with a simple, "Hi, I'm [your name here]." Don't drop some witty pickup line that you read on a friend's status update. They don't work. Stick with what you know . . . like your name.

STEP 5 **Give her a genuine compliment.**

This requires you to really mean what you say and say what you mean. If you fake this part, she will know. Don't ask how, girls just seem to know when guys are not being authentic. Try giving her a compliment like one of these, if appropriate:

- "I went to your volleyball game yesterday. You really did well."
- "Good work in class today. You made answering those lab questions look so easy."
- "Your new hairstyle looks good. I like it."

STEP 6 **Talk *with* her, not to her.**

This means you are both talking, in a conversation. Your best bet to get the conversation started is to ask her questions that require more than a simple yes or no answer. Look for a conversation topic *she* would be interested in talking about. Keep asking thoughtful questions and practice being a good listener. If she is into the conversation, she will also ask you questions. When she does, don't brag, go off topic, or talk about yourself too much. Keep the conversation light and focused on her.

STEP 7 **End the conversation well.**

Wrap things up with a positive statement like, "It was good talking with you. I look forward to seeing you again soon." Now is a good time to ask her for her cell number.

Did You Know?

Men's brains release "feel-good" chemicals when playing video games, laughing, and engaging in physical activity. Women's brains do the same, but theirs release these feel-good chemicals when engaging in a meaningful conversation. So go talk with her, and her brain will love it.

Invite a Girl on a First Date

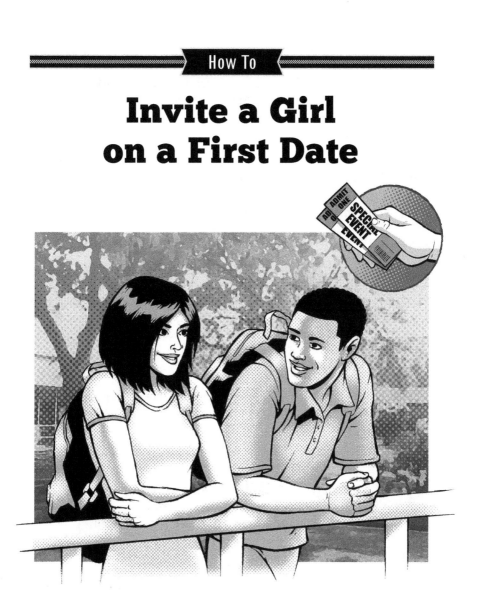

YOU WILL NEED:

- A girl you want to ask on a date
- Confidence
- Fresh breath
  (see "How to Freshen Bad Breath")

TIME REQUIRED:

- It may seem longer than it actually takes.

Prepare yourself. What you are about to attempt may end up ranking in the top 10 most memorable moments of your life. The first date invite story will be told for years to come and from two perspectives, yours and hers. How you plan and undertake this asking determines if the story told will be epic or horrific.

STEP 1 **Choose carefully.**

A date is about getting to know somebody better. Dating will help you learn what type of girl you are interested in and what type of girl is interested in you.

STEP 2 **Pick an event.**

She is more likely to say yes to a date if you have a specific event in mind. Think of something she would be interested in doing with you.

STEP 3 **Plan your transportation.**

Avoid long rides, as they are not usually first-date friendly.

STEP 4 **Plan your ask.**

Give her at least two or three days between asking and when you plan on going out. If you want the date to be on Friday, ask her on Tuesday or Wednesday. She may need to ask her parents, and anticipation is half the fun of a good first date.

STEP 5 **Ask her out.**

Timing and approach is everything. With confidence describe your plans and ask if she would like to join you. Always ask her in person! Never ask a girl out with a text.

Wise Guy

There is no guarantee she will say yes to a date with you. What is guaranteed is if you never ask, she will never say yes.

Plan a Date

YOU WILL NEED:
- A girl who said yes to a date with you
- Confidence
- Cash
- Transportation

TIME REQUIRED:
- 1 hour of planning

Guys who are mature enough to start dating know the following truth: girls like a man with a plan. So what's your plan, man? If you want a date to go great, you will need to put some thought and energy in before you go out. The best way to assure she text-brags to her friends that she's "hagt" (having a good time) is to dedicate some T.I.M.E. to planning and preparing the date. Here's how.

STEP 1 **T**hink it.

Try to think about the date from her perspective. What would she like to do? What do you have in common?

STEP 2 **L**ink it.

Write down your date ideas on a piece of paper. Brainstorming is a creative way to test an idea, see potential conflicts, and identify your best options. Consider costs, transportation, timing, and perhaps even getting her/your parents' permission.

STEP 3 **M**ap it.

Once you have your best idea written down, map out your plan.

- When is the date?—Day, evening, night?
- When does the date begin?—She needs a specific time to expect your arrival.
- What is your budget?—A date can get expensive, so set a budget and stick to it.
- Who is paying?—Going "dutch" is good if you want to keep things simple. (See "How to Decide Who Pays on a Date")
- Where are you going?—Be specific. For example, plan for dinner at [**fill in the location**] vs. finding a place.
- How will you get there?—Will you meet her there? Will you pick her up? Will you be driving?
- When does the date end?—Have her home on time. Be specific and honor your commitment. This is one way you will gain her favor and the trust of her parents.

STEP 4 **E**arn it.

Girls like a man with a plan and a man who can take action. So lead the way and have a fun date. Hopefully she will appreciate the effort.

Did You Know?

Many states have laws for new drivers restricting unrelated passengers and driving during certain hours of the night. If you will be driving, know the laws before a police officer explains them to you, in front of your date.

Decide Who Pays on a Date

YOU WILL NEED:
- A planned date
- Money

TIME REQUIRED:
- 1-minute conversation

Dating etiquette established over a century ago is becoming ancient history. Back in the day, the guy paid for everything on a date. Today's modern man is challenged to make the change as the modern woman often wants to pay for some or even all of a date. So who picks up the tab? He? She? We? Here is a simple and respectful way to determine who opens their wallet without opening a can of controversy.

STEP 1 **Who asked who?**

If you ask her, you need to make a good first impression. Gentlemen's rule: Always pay on the first date. No matter the circumstances. If she asked you, and you said yes, still offer to follow the gentlemen's rule.

STEP 2 **Second date.**

If she extends the invitation to pay for something, consider it. She may want to show she doesn't expect you to go broke and that she can contribute some cash too. This is a good sign. She may be a keeper.

STEP 3 **Dates three and beyond.**

Sounds like you may be on your way to having an official girlfriend. If you are not sure yet, wait a few more dates, then think about having the D.T.R. talk (see "How to Talk Like a Man"). Once you have determined that, yep, she's your girlfriend, keep the money-spending lines of communication open. The word **girlfriend** is a compound word uniting "girl" with "friend." True friends complement each other in all areas, including money. Talk about it and work together to spend and pay appropriately while dating.

Man Fact or Fiction:
I can't afford to date.

Fiction. The fact is, you can't put a price on love, but you can on a date. You don't have to spend big CA$H to show a girl you're creative, considerate, and worth going on date #2 with next week. Dates should be fun, not de**fun**ding.

Meet a Girl's Parents for the First Time

YOU WILL NEED:
- Solid handshake
- Clean clothes
- Smile
- Manners

TIME REQUIRED:
- 1–5 minutes

Few things will scare you more than meeting a girl's parents for the first time. This first impression can set their expectation of whether or not you can be trusted with their little girl. Get this introduction right and you will be one step closer to gaining her parents' trust.

STEP 1 **Make eye contact.**

When greeting her parents, look them in the eyes. Comfortable eye contact is 4–5 seconds, pause by briefly looking away, and then make eye contact again.

STEP 2 **Smile.**

An authentic smile conveys optimism and high levels of confidence.

STEP 3 **Speak with confidence.**

Starting with her mom, say something simple yet polite, like, "Nice to meet you, Mrs. [last name] and Mr. [last name]."

STEP 4 **Shake hands.**

Follow the "How to Shake Hands" steps. By extending a friendly and traditional greeting, you show them you are respectful and know how to interact with adults.

STEP 5 **Compliment their daughter.**

Say something nice about their daughter that has nothing to do with the way she looks or how excited you are to be going out with her.

STEP 6 **Use your manners.**

Say "please," "thank you," "yes" rather than "yeah," "no" rather than "nah," and "excuse me?" rather than "huh?" Open doors for others, chew with your mouth closed, don't talk about yourself too much, and by all means, control your bodily functions.

More Info

A good dad protects his daughter. Any guys trying to date his daughter can be seen as public enemy #1. The trick to gaining Dad's approval is to treat his daughter with the respect he wants for his little girl. Think of it like Dad is watching, at all times. This will keep you off his "Most Deadly" list and increase the odds of you gaining an elevated spot on his daughter's "Most Wanted" list.

Balance Time with Girlfriend vs. Guy Friends

YOU WILL NEED:
- Guy friends
- Girlfriend

TIME REQUIRED:
- Daily life

If your guy friends ever say, "Man, where have you been? It's like you've abandoned us for her," then you are officially out of balance in the time you spend with your girlfriend versus guy friends. Some guys make the mistake of spending every minute with their girlfriend. Before school, between classes, at lunch, after school, on weekends, texting, talking, online . . . you get the idea. Simply put, men know balance is best, and here is how you can show your guy friends and girlfriend they are both an important part of your life.

STEP 1 **Don't smother each other.**

The fastest way to drive a girl away is to take up all her free time. There is truth in the old saying, "Absence makes the heart grow fonder."

STEP 2 **Plan time together.**

Once a week take the T.I.M.E. to plan a date with your girlfriend, just the two of you. A date doesn't have to be grand or expensive. Think fun. (See "How to Plan a Date")

STEP 3 **Mix it up.**

You should be able to hang out with both your guy friends and your girlfriend at the same time. Equally sharing time within a group of friends is a sign of maturity.

STEP 4 **Plan time apart.**

You have your friends and she has hers. Maintaining friendships that were formed B.G. (before girlfriend) is important to your social health. Treat your friends right, and they'll still be there for you A.G.

Man Fact or Fiction:
Bro-mances come before romances.

Fact—if you are planning on living with your best guy friends the rest of your life, then yes, choose your bro's first. If not, then . . .

Fiction. The fact is, true bro's are good for now, yet one day you and a very special lady will choose to get married and put each other first, over all others.

Respectfully Break Up with a Girl

YOU WILL NEED:
- Empathy
  (see glossary)
- Quiet, semi-private to private location

TIME REQUIRED:
- 30 minutes

This may hurt a little. Actually this may hurt a lot. Either way it must be done. So how do you go about breaking up with a girl when you think she is a good person but just not a good match for you? You are closer to knowing the answer than you may think. Consider this. Respect her just as you would want to be respected if she were the one ending the relationship.

STEP 1 Consider your words.

Know what you are going to say before you talk with her. Practice if you need to.

STEP 2 Pick the place.

Decide where you will talk with her in person, face-to-face. Pick a place private enough that she can avoid the embarrassment of other people witnessing her emotions. Never break up via a text message or on social media.

STEP 3 Timing is everything.

Seldom is there a "good" time to break up, but don't make the situation worse by ending things right before or during an important event.

STEP 4 Respect her feelings.

She may respond with sadness and tears, surprise and frustration, or she may even get mad and hurl accusations at you. The only person you can control is you; so keep your cool, let her respond as she chooses, and respect her feelings.

STEP 5 Keep it positive.

Following your breakup only speak of the good aspects of your relationship. You two shared some good times, so honor those memories and talk publicly only about the positive. If you don't have anything good to say about her, don't say anything at all.

Did You Know?

Neil Sedaka's 1962 song "Breaking Up Is Hard to Do" hit #1 on the Billboard Hot 100. Since its debut last century, the heartbreak song has been rerecorded by more than 32 professional artists. It just goes to show that time doesn't change the fact that breaking up is hard to do.

SOCIAL SKILLS & MANNERS

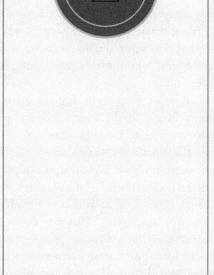

2

It's remarkable! The surge of social media sources has grown from a surfable wave to a virtual tsunami. Just as one "like my status update" site rises in popularity, another "share this picture instantly" app drowns it out. People can tag, comment, post, repost, link, and follow their growing collection of "friends" with near hoarder quantities. Some even believe one space is too restricting and take great pride in checking in on multiple social sites just to make sure they are not missing anything, or being missed. With heads down and eyes locked on HD pixels, many guys are failing to see the importance of the social skills required to update their face-to-face connections with the people standing right beside them.

Learning the craft of meeting, properly greeting, and truly getting to know people expands a man's social network and adds value to both his personal and professional life. One man who has mastered this craft of staying connected is public relations and marketing guru George Toles. With a voice for broadcasting and a magnetic personality, George seldom finds himself in a place where he doesn't know anybody. His openness to and interest in others has built him an extensive network of authentic relationships in countries, communities, companies, organizations, and churches around the world.

George's secret to making so many friends is simple: "I introduce myself, look them in the eye, shake their hand, and pay close attention to what matters most to them. Do they share stories about their kids, work, sports, or do they just want to talk about themselves? I ask them meaningful questions about their family, friendships, and their faith. I try to listen and make connections."[1] Once George discovers a connection, he introduces his new friend to another of his friends with similar interests, needs, and opportunities. "This way they can make, expand, and strengthen their connection with other people. That and introducing them takes the burden off me of having to constantly keep up with them. Once I have made an introduction, I exit stage right, quickly."

George has proven that a valuable network is founded on building meaningful relationships with reliable people, then serving and staying in touch with them, seeking to regularly add value to their lives. He has followed this path to build a good reputation in business, to heal and protect family ties, and to make legions of friends around the world. Best of all, George takes his networking gift a step further. "When people know they can trust me to introduce them to helpful friends, they are open to meeting my best Friend, who is the wisest, most loyal, patient, forgiving, influential, and welcoming Person I know."

Meet George Toles

Founder of His Deal (www.hisdeal.org), George Toles has been a deejay, newscaster, TV sports anchor, program director, radio salesman, recording studio manager, commercial narrator, NBA stadium announcer, ad agency owner, and mentor to many good men.

Shake Hands

YOU WILL NEED:
- Clean hands
- Authentic smile
- Confidence

TIME REQUIRED:
- 3 seconds

Shaking hands is an important part of making a good first impression. The palm-pressing tradition started back in medieval times as a way of showing that neither greeter held a concealed weapon. The tradition holds true today for those who grasp the significance of trust, respect, and honor. Mastering the handshake is one way to show new acquaintances, teachers, bosses, and your girlfriend's parents that you are friendly, confident, and respectful.

STEP 1 **Make eye contact.**

Look the person in the eyes as you prepare to shake their hand. Just don't lock on with a creepy, wide-eyed stare.

STEP 2 **Prepare to shake.**

Extend your right arm and hand toward the other person. With your hand open and your thumb pointing upward, direct your handshake to align with the center of your body.

STEP 3 **Meet in the middle.**

Keeping your extended arm slightly bent at the elbow, meet the other person's hand in the space half the distance between your body and theirs. The flat of your palm should meet theirs with fingers extended and thumb raised.

STEP 4 **Grasp hands.**

Use slight pressure to give their hand a firm but gentle squeeze. No limp fish, wimpy handshakes allowed! (Hint: Pretend their hand is a small bird that needs to be held firmly enough to not fly away but not so tightly it is crushed.)

STEP 5 **Shake hands.**

With your wrist locked, raise your hand upward about two inches and downward about two inches. One or two upward and downward shakes should be sufficient.

STEP 6 **Release hands.**

Simultaneously let go and lower your hand back to your side. Do not wipe your hand on your pants, even if their palm was sweaty.

More Info

In many cultures, making eye contact is a sign of interest and respect. In others, looking into the eyes is a sign of disrespect and even lust. Know what the traditions are where you are. As the saying goes, "When in Rome, do as the Romans do." *(Just an FYI: When shaking hands in Rome, be sure to maintain eye contact while greeting people. Otherwise Italians may think you are hiding something.)*

Introduce Yourself

YOU WILL NEED:
- Confident handshake
- Friendly smile

TIME REQUIRED:
- 30 seconds

Sometimes you just have to put yourself out there. Instead of waiting for people to come and introduce themselves to you, get proactive and make the introduction yourself. Your confident personal introduction communicates your openness to meeting new people and interest in expanding your real-world social network.

STEP 1 **Approach with confidence.**

Keep your shoulders back and head up when approaching the person you want to meet.

STEP 2 **Smile.**

A friendly smile makes for a great first impression.

STEP 3 **Make eye contact.**

Look them in the eyes, yet don't lock in too strong with a creepy stare down.

STEP 4 **Meet and greet.**

Just prior to offering a friendly handshake, meet the other person with a greeting that includes your name, possible connection, and reason for your introducing yourself.

Example:

"Hello. I'd like to introduce myself. My name is Aaron and I believe you work with my dad. He tells me you attended the same university I am considering. May I ask you a few questions about why you chose that school and your experience there?"

STEP 5 **Shake hands.**

Extending a confident handshake is both a respectful and professional way of showing you are an open and friendly person. (See "How to Shake Hands")

Wise Guy

"Expanding your real-world social network with real friends is nothing like collecting virtual friends online. Real friends are people you actually know, people who you actually interact with in real and meaningful ways. Surrounded by real friends, a man can do about anything."

—George Toles

Introduce Other People

YOU WILL NEED:

- Two or more people needing an introduction
- Their full names locked in your memory
- Some positive information to share about each person

TIME REQUIRED:

- 2 minutes

Properly introducing two or more people is an important skill to learn. When people you know also know each other, you gain a reputation as a connector. Men who are connectors keep introductions comfortable and never create a situation that obligates people to start a friendship. If they hit it off, that's great. Thanks for the introduction.

STEP 1 **Show respect.**

If there are ladies in the group, begin with them. Start by introducing the senior person and then the person they are with. Work your way down to the youngest person.

STEP 2 **Use full names.**

Whenever possible, introduce people using both their first and last name.

Example:
"Coach, I'd like to introduce you to my dad, Robert Catherman." Next, turning the introduction to your coach, "Dad, this is Coach Chris Moore."

STEP 3 **Share something personal.**

People want to know and be known, so say something positive and personal about the people you are introducing to demonstrate that you value them.

Example:
Starting with Dad: "Coach, did you know my dad hasn't missed a single one of my games in two years?" Now turn the focus to your coach: "Dad, you will be proud to learn that Coach Moore graduated from the same university as you, where he was an all-American athlete."

STEP 4 **Restate names.**

By stating and restating people's names in your introduction, you help others better remember the people they are meeting.

STEP 5 **Set up the win-win.**

Always try to show a good reason why the people you are introducing could find value in knowing each other.

Example:
"Coach Moore, I remember you telling us to focus on keeping our grades up the second half of the season. Well, my dad is an engineer and is pretty good at helping me with my math homework. He is willing to tutor our guys twice a week, if that would help."

STEP 6 **Step back.**

Now that the personal introductions are done, let people talk. You set them up with names, personal information, and a win-win opportunity. Now let them take the next steps.

Man Fact or Fiction:
Sticking your tongue out can be polite.

Fact. When in Tibet, it is good manners to poke your tongue out when being introduced. The tradition dates back to the ninth century when a cruel Tibetan king named Lang Darma was discovered to have a black tongue. People hated the king and feared meeting his reincarnation. Following his death they started sticking out their tongues when greeting to prove they weren't the king, version 2.0.

Open the Door for Another Person

YOU WILL NEED:
- Hinged door

TIME REQUIRED:
- 5 seconds

Whether you are practicing your gentlemanly ways or being polite, opening the door for another person is a good way of showing both respect and consideration to those you know and total strangers. Such an act of kindness will be appreciated by both your girlfriend and boss, and can literally and figuratively help "open doors" for you in the future. Yet getting it right all hinges on knowing why, when, and how to push, pull, or step through.

STEP 1 **Know why and when.**

Why? Because you are a considerate, respectful, patient, thoughtful, humble, and all-around good man who treats other people like he wants to be treated. When? Whenever your sister, mom, grandma, girlfriend, or her sister, mom, grandma, or for that matter when anybody's sister, mother, and grandma is going through the same door as you. For your boss, co-workers, and customers. For your coach, teacher, principal, substitute, janitor, and especially the lunch lady. Basically, open the door for anybody you have an opportunity to serve.

STEP 2 **Identify which way the door opens.**

Right or left, in or out? Look at the handle and hinges: for example, if the hinges are visible and the handle is on the right, the door swings out toward you and to the left. No visible hinges means you'll push to open. A push bar across the door tells you to, well . . . push.

STEP 3 **Arrive early.**

You need to arrive a step or two before the other person. Avoid reaching around them to open the door. This crowds the space, forcing the other person to awkwardly step away from you.

STEP 4 **Open the door.**

When you pull the door open, allow the other person to walk through first and then follow. When you push, walk through first and hold it open until the other person has passed and is safely clear of the door.

STEP 5 **Don't leave them waiting.**

You are not obligated to hold the door for every person behind you. Holding it open for a few people is nice, yet being the doorman for a line of strangers is usually a paid position. And it's rude to leave the person with you waiting on the other side. So let the door close when there are a few steps between you and the next guy headed for the door.

Did You Know?

Automatic door openers have been around for more than 2,000 years. The Greek scholar Heron of Alexandria, also known as . . . wait for it . . . "Hero," was a mathematician, engineer, and author credited with inventing the earliest known automatic door opener. He brilliantly built a series of hydraulically driven weights, ropes, and pulleys to open the city gates and temple doors just as the people were arriving first thing in the day.

Set a Table

YOU WILL NEED:
- Plates
- Silverware
- Glasses
- Napkins

TIME REQUIRED:
- 30 seconds per setting

Get set to sit down. While delivery dining is fun for sofa surfing gamers and sports fans alike, other meals taste best when eaten at the table. By setting the table, you provide a casual way to invite family and friends to sit down and savor the flavor of time spent together over some good food.

STEP 1 **Place the dinner plate.**

Set the dinner plate about one inch in from the table's edge, directly in front of where the person will be seated.

STEP 2 **Place the side plate.**

If salad or bread will be served, place the smaller side plate to the upper left of the dinner plate.

STEP 3 **Set the forks.**

Forks are set one inch to the left of the plate. The dinner fork is placed closest to the plate and smaller salad fork to the left of the dinner fork.

STEP 4 **Set the knife.**

Knives are set one inch to the right of the plate. Position the cutting edge toward the plate.

STEP 5 **Set the spoon.**

Spoons are set to the right of the knife.

STEP 6 **Set the water glass.**

Water glasses are set to the upper right of the plate, above the knife.

STEP 7 **Set the napkin.**

Napkins are set to the left of the forks.

STEP 8 **Set another place.**

Space each additional place setting about 24 inches apart.

Wise Guy

"Your girlfriend's parents know some tricky testing techniques to see if you are good enough for their daughter. One way is to invite you over for dinner and then ask you to help set the table. The simple fact that you know on which sides the fork and knife are set will impress them. That and chewing with your mouth closed."

—Jonathan

Order from a Menu

YOU WILL NEED:
- Restaurant
- Menu

TIME REQUIRED:
- 3 minutes

No more ordering by numbers. Any guy can pick a supersized #3 from a wall-mounted picture-perfect menu. It's time to man up, sit down, spread a cloth napkin on your lap, and order from a menu held in your hands. It's true: menu dining requires more time and preparation. The good thing is, so does the meal you will enjoy. Add to the experience ambiance, friends, and three courses of food you can savor, and you may discover ordering from a menu is your new #1 favorite way to eat out.

STEP 1 **Order drinks.**

Your first consideration will be beverages. Always start by giving the ladies' drink orders to your server first. If water is desired, order it now, as some restaurants will not serve it unless requested.

STEP 2 **Review menu.**

Look the entire menu over. The first listings are usually starters or appetizers. Next come entrées or main courses and side dishes. Finally desserts are offered toward the end of the menu. Try to narrow down your choices before the server takes your orders.

STEP 3 **Pair appetizers.**

If an appetizer looks good, ask those dining with you if they too would enjoy anything pre-meal. Pair your selection with the tastes of all who wish to share.

STEP 4 **Ask about specials.**

Ask your server for today's specials. After the dish descriptions have been given, ask for the price of any specials you find appetizing. Remember specials can be more expensive than the menu's daily entrées.

STEP 5 **Order entrées.**

Ladies first, tell your server what your entrée selection will be for dinner. Be sure to have read and selected which side dishes come with your meal. If a salad is included in your selection, choose what type of dressing you would like served.

STEP 6 **Consider dessert.**

Once your meal is complete, consider ordering dessert. In most restaurants it is acceptable to share a single serving of dessert between two people.

Man Fact or Fiction:

Restaurant menus can make you sick.

Fact. You may read a restaurant menu and think, "Yuck! That poached fish and string squash special looks sickening." But have you ever considered that the menu you are holding could actually make you puke? Few restaurants clean their menus between customers. That means other diners' dirty hands held that same menu you are holding now. You follow them, touch your food, and put that food in your mouth. Holding a menu can't be avoided, but keeping it from touching your plate or silverware can be done. That and seriously consider washing your hands after ordering.

Leave a Tip

YOU WILL NEED:
- Good service
- Money

TIME REQUIRED:
- 30 seconds

The practice of offering gratuity has been part of the hospitality industry for a few hundred years. Gratuity is also called a tip—think of the acronym "to insure promptitude." A few hundred years ago, a tip was given before service to ensure faster and better care was given to those who tipped over those who didn't. Today a tip is given after service in appreciation for prompt attention and good service.

STEP 1 **Assess service.**

Consider the quality of the service you were provided. Was it below, average, or above the standard you expected?

STEP 2 **Do the math.**

An average tip for average service is 15% of the pre-tax bill before any discounts or coupons are applied. This means when your pre-tax bill is $25.00, the tip is $3.75.

Below average = 10%
Average = 15%
Above average = 20%

STEP 3 **Leave the tip.**

When you pay, add the tip to your final bill. If you are paying with cash, leave the cash tip sitting on the table.

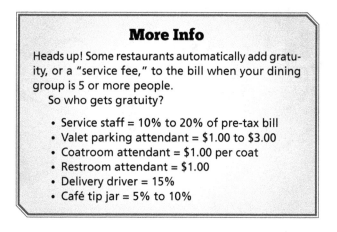

More Info

Heads up! Some restaurants automatically add gratuity, or a "service fee," to the bill when your dining group is 5 or more people.
So who gets gratuity?

- Service staff = 10% to 20% of pre-tax bill
- Valet parking attendant = $1.00 to $3.00
- Coatroom attendant = $1.00 per coat
- Restroom attendant = $1.00
- Delivery driver = 15%
- Café tip jar = 5% to 10%

Wrap a Gift

YOU WILL NEED:
- Gift
- Box for gift
- Event-appropriate wrapping paper
- Tape
- Scissors
- Ribbon or peel-and-stick bow

TIME REQUIRED:
- 5 minutes

Well, my intentions were good" is an excuse joke for the poorly wrapped gift. Dude, no! Presentation is important. A well-wrapped present will be admired and complimented prior to the paper peeling. Wrap a gift just right, and often the receiver (especially girls) will save the perfect paper as a memento of your thoughtfulness. This is good. With a few quick tips and a little practice, you too can elevate your wrapping from wasteful to wow.

STEP 1 **Gather your materials.**

On a flat surface, gather your gift, box, wrapping paper, tape, ribbon, and scissors.

STEP 2 **Box the gift.**

Place the gift in a like-sized box. If the item is fragile, be sure to cushion it inside the box.

STEP 3 **Measure wrapping paper.**

Unroll the wrapping paper to measure a few inches longer than the distance around the box.

STEP 4 **Cut wrapping paper.**

Use scissors to cut the wrapping paper free from the roll. Cut as straight as you can.

STEP 5 **Trim wrapping paper.**

Cut the sides of the paper so they will fold up a little less than the height of the box's ends.

STEP 6 **Wrap four sides.**

Place the gift box upside down in the center of the wrapping paper. Bring one long end of the paper up and over the box. Secure the end of the paper with tape just past the center of the bottom of the box. Repeat on the other side with the addition of folding over the very end of the paper to hide the cut edge.

STEP 7 **Wrap one end.**

Pick one of the two open ends and fold the paper down to meet the side of the box. This will create two paper triangles on either side. Fold the triangles in and secure them with tape. Now bring up the remaining flap of paper, fold over the end, and tape.

STEP 8 **Wrap remaining end.**

Repeat STEP 7 on the other end of the box.

STEP 9 **Add bow or ribbon.**

Finish off the gift-wrapping with a decorative peel-and-stick bow or, if you're up to the challenge, first wrap it neatly with a ribbon and then complete it with a handmade bow.

Wise Guy

"I bought my brother some gift wrap for Christmas.
I took it to the gift wrap department and told them
to wrap it, but in a different print so he would know
when to stop unwrapping."

—Steven Wright,
American comedian, actor, and writer

Clean a Bathroom

YOU WILL NEED:

- Rubber gloves
- Shower cleaner
- Window cleaner
- Toilet bowl cleaner
- Disinfectant cleaner
- Toilet bowl brush
- Microfiber cloths or paper towels
- Broom & dustpan
- Floor cleaner
- Mop & bucket

TIME REQUIRED:

- 15–30 minutes

Your house may be your castle, but the cleanliness of your throne is the true expression of your reign. How you clean and keep your bathroom will either impress or disgust your guests. They may or may not look in your medicine cabinet for clues about your personal life, but they are guaranteed to see the ring in the toilet and dried toothpaste splatter on the mirror. Cleaning your bathroom is not only healthy, it's a good way to keep your housekeeping reputation out of the toilet.

STEP 1 **Tidy the bathroom.**

Remove everything that does not belong in the bathroom and return it to its proper place.

STEP 2 **Scrub the shower and bathtub.**

Remove everything from the shower and spray it with shower cleaner. Scrub the walls and the basin in a circular motion from top to bottom. Spray the entire area with water to rinse off the cleaner, and wipe it down again with a damp cloth. Be sure to clean your faucet and showerhead as well.

STEP 3 **Clean the toilet.**

Wearing rubber gloves, pour toilet bowl cleaner around the rim of the toilet. Use the toilet bowl brush and scrub around the whole inside of the toilet, including under the rim. Use the disinfectant cleaner to spray the entire outside of the toilet, including the handle, top of toilet, and under the toilet seat. Using a paper towel, wipe down every surface on your toilet. Take off the gloves before continuing to clean the rest of the bathroom.

STEP 4 **Shine the mirror.**

Using window cleaner, spray down your mirror and wipe it with a fresh cloth or paper towels.

STEP 5 **Wipe the countertops.**

Use a disinfectant cleaner to spray down the countertops, sink, fixtures, and faucets. Using a clean cloth or paper towel, wipe down all surfaces right away to prevent spotting or streaking.

STEP 6 **Clean the floors.**

Starting from the farthest corner of the room, sweep and then mop toward the door.

STEP 7 **Take out the trash.**

Empty the trash can and make sure that the inside of the can is clean.

Did You Know?

Close the toilet lid before you flush. When the water rushes into the bowl, droplets of toilet water, urine, and feces become airborne. For this exact reason, put your toothbrush in a drawer or keep it as far away from the toilet as possible.

Make a Bed

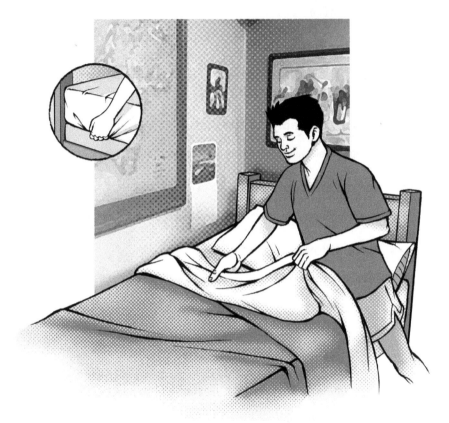

YOU WILL NEED:
- Fitted bottom sheet
- Flat sheet
- Blanket or comforter
- Pillows
- Pillowcases

TIME REQUIRED:
- 1–3 minutes

Why should a guy make his bed when he's just going to get back in it later? Because a real man's room looks neat—not like you thrashed your way through a bad dream all night. It takes only a minute to make your bed, and the result is way better than your friends seeing your drool-stained pillow and collectors edition space droid sheets. Yeah, yeah, we know. You've had them since you were a kid. Well, maybe it's time to man up, get a new comforter, and start making your bed.

STEP 1 Fit the bottom sheet.

Take the fitted sheet and pull the elastic corners down and over each corner of the mattress.

STEP 2 Spread the top sheet.

The top of the flat sheet has a wide hem and should align even with the top of the bed, while the bottom of the sheet should hang off the foot of the bed.

STEP 3 Tuck in the top sheet.

At the foot of the bed, lift one mattress corner to tuck the bottom length of sheet into the space between the mattress and box spring. Repeat this process for the other corner.

STEP 4 (OPTIONAL) Spread your blanket.

If you like additional layers of warmth on the bed, repeat STEP 3 with a light blanket.

STEP 5 Spread the comforter.

Make sure both sides and bottom of the comforter drape evenly over the bed.

STEP 6 Place pillows.

Put the pillowcases on the pillows. Fluff the pillows and place them at the top of your bed.

More Info

It's a good practice to replace your pillow every year. The fact is that within 2 years of nightly use, one-third of your pillow's weight consists of dead skin and dust mites and their droppings. Nasty! So get a new pillow and you really will sleep tight—don't let the bedbugs bite.

WORK & ETHICS

3

"Choose a job you love, and you will never have to work a day in your life," said the Chinese philosopher Confucius more than 2,500 years ago. His words have stuck around since the fifth century BC because they are true. Going to work is a good thing when a man loves what he does. So how does a guy find a job he loves so much that it's not work? The answer can be found in the modern-day wisdom shared by five super competitive best friends who love to step up, take their shot, and make every day on the job count.

Meet Dude Perfect. Twin brothers Cory and Coby Cotton, Garrett Hilbert, Cody Jones, Tyler Toney, and their supercool mascot, Panda. These five guys and their bear have loved to play/work since way back in the day when they were roommates at Texas A&M University. Known today across the universe as simply Dude Perfect, the guys have transformed their love for backyard trick shots into a business with bragging rights that include a TV show, book, and game, all wrapped up in one of YouTube's most popular brands. Sporting a "failure is not an option" attitude, their business is to impress, and business is booming with millions of subscribers and billions of views. Yes, you read right, billions of views! That's Billion with a capital *B* and count them: , , , , four commas.

The trick to Dude Perfect turning their viral videos into a wildly successful business plan isn't the once-in-a-lifetime shot you'd expect. Any dude can follow the same five principles Dude Perfect shoots for both on the job and in life. So what are these five principles, you ask? According to Cory Cotton, the trick to "Making Your Shot Count" is to *get excited, own it, blink later, inspire others*, and *give back*.

First things first: you have to **get excited** about something. Cory says,

What gets us excited is coming into work and trying to create content that puts smiles on people's faces. We feel there is a huge role model gap in entertainment today. Unfortunately, there's also a male gap right now. We focus on being positive male role models, and not just to guys. Girls watch our videos and television shows too. We want people to see there is a different way to live and have fun besides just pitching the party scene. You can have fun doing sports and being competitive. So, what gets us super excited about work is creating new content that makes people smile in a way most mainstream media and entertainment don't.[1]

Dude Perfect's principle to *get excited* is something you should consider working with too. To find your *get excited* thing, Cory suggests you ask yourself a couple questions:

First, have you paid enough attention to the things that excite you? Have you taken notice of the moments that are awesome—like *really awesome*? And second, what are those things? What is it that thrills you? What is it that's almost unnaturally exciting to you?[2]

Next, you'll have to **own it,** and not just a little bit. To make that big shot you'll have to be all in, plus some. Cory explains,

For our work at Dude Perfect we have never been able to shake the belief that "idea" drives everything. If an idea doesn't get you excited, then it's probably not worth pursuing. For Dude Perfect to *Own It*, we start with a great idea worth giving 110% to make happen. This is important because it takes a lot of effort to pull off something that's truly amazing. It takes time and patience, and unfortunately, that's more than most people are willing to commit. You can't be out for instant gratification. We've made some shots on the first try, but usually we have to try again and again before making it. In our work we've had to put in the time to accomplish something fun for people to watch. That starts with owning an idea worth pursuing and then giving it 110% until it's accomplished.[3]

To accomplish your big ideas you'll need to get moving. It's a fast-paced world out there, so don't blink or you might miss an opportunity. In fact, **blink later** is the next principle Dude Perfect follows. Cory shares this wise advice in his book *Go Big* when he writes,

Don't talk yourself out of a Go Big idea by sitting for too long. Again don't blink. Act.[4]

It takes a lot to Go Big with your ideas, so maybe it's a good thing that most people don't make their big shot on the first try, or all on their own. The Dude Perfect guys know the importance of surrounding themselves with people who support them when opportunity knocks and celebrating together when something amazing happens. The trick is to act on your opportunities without taking advantage of the people involved. Cory talks about putting that belief into practice:

> Opportunities come up all the time and we need to take advantage of the right ones, but never by taking advantage of people. One thing we [Dude Perfect] have come to know is all those things people chase, be it fame, money, or power, none of them are eternal. Those things fade. But to get that stuff, some people are willing to take advantage of others by stabbing them in the back. That's the exact opposite of how we want to handle ourselves. We want to put out the biggest and best videos anyone has ever seen, but we'll never undercut people to do it.[5]

Seriously! Are these guys too good to be true? How can they sink the most impossible trick shots ever and focus on treating people right, all at the same time? Well, despite what the trolls and haters say, Dude Perfect doesn't fake any shots, and that includes the shot they are taking on you. Believe it or not, Dude Perfect believes in you and your Go Big dream. So much so that **inspire others** is the next principle they shoot for.

> At the end of the day, you've got two options: achieve temporary results by persuading others, or focus on inspiring others and create lasting momentum, positively impacting those you reach. Choose the second option. It does take effort, but as you'll soon see, the results far outweigh the work.[6]

Who has inspired these dudes to work so hard at inspiring others? Cory says, "Guys like Tim Tebow who have pushed to excellence and remained strong in their faith. Rob Dyrdek for staying relevant and fun. And of course we're all huge Stephen Curry fans." Just as the Dude Perfect guys are inspired and inspiring, you too can work hard to rally people, create momentum, and inspire others. Showing people you believe in them is how to keep the job work fun and feeling like it's not work at all.

Finally, the guys all believe that to those dudes who are given much, much is expected of those dudes. This shows in their fifth principle, **give back**. Over the years Dude Perfect has worked alongside charities like Compassion International and the Make-A-Wish Foundation. Yet having a *give back* mindset isn't about charity; it's about having an others-centered perspective.

> For us giving back is a mindset and different than just giving to charity every once in a while. For us it's been a really healthy thing to mentor younger guys. My brother and I have been doing life with the same group of guys since they were in sixth grade. To have twenty guys who remind us constantly—and

everybody needs to be reminded—that life isn't just about you is a good thing. The thing we will hang our hat on at the end of the day is that spending an entire life chasing after popularity, fame, money, and power is shallow, because all those things fade away. Instead, the five of us dudes have found real and lasting joy in our faith. For us to build that into the lives of the twenty guys closest to us, that is where we can make the greatest impact. And who knows how far the ripples of that impact will go in their lives.[7]

Confucius probably never competed in an epic trick shot battle with other philosophers, but his wisdom about loving your job is still amazing to see in action. If five best friends and a Panda can make a job out of sinking trick shots by practicing the principles *get excited, own it, blink later, inspire others,* and *give back,* then you can too. So step up, take the shot, and make it count.

OOOHHHHH!!!!!!!!
Pound it, Noggin!

Meet Dude Perfect

To learn more about Dude Perfect, read their book *Go Big* and visit them online at dudeperfect.com.

Apply for a Job

YOU WILL NEED:
- Job application
- Résumé and cover letter
- Telephone

TIME REQUIRED:
- Varies

> Hard work spotlights the character of people:
> some turn up their sleeves, some turn up their noses,
> and some don't turn up at all.
>
> —Sam Ewing, former professional baseball player with
> the Chicago White Sox & Toronto Blue Jays

STEP 1 **Contact the employer.**

Call the employer and inquire about any job openings. If there are opportunities available, clarify how you can apply. Be sure to write down the name of the hiring manager so future correspondences can be directed to the appropriate person.

STEP 2 **Fill out an application.**

Many companies now require prospective employees to fill out applications online. Some may ask you to pick up an application in person, so be sure to dress appropriately. Fill out the application in its entirety. (See "How to Fill Out an Application")

STEP 3 **Construct a résumé.**

If necessary, prepare a résumé and cover letter to include with the submission of your application.

STEP 4 **Proofread.**

Be sure to edit and proofread your résumé, cover letter, and application prior to submission to ensure they are free of errors. This is critical in making a good impression on the hiring manager.

STEP 5 **Submit your application.**

Whenever possible, turn in your completed application IN PERSON (unless the employer will accept only online submissions). Dress and act professionally to ensure you make a good first impression. Remember, dressing professionally means wearing clothes appropriate for the job the way the employer wants rather than wearing your clothes any way you want on the job.

STEP 6 **Follow up.**

Several days after submitting your application, visit the employer and ask to speak with the hiring manager IN PERSON. Confirm that your application was received and reviewed, and always be prepared to answer the hiring manager's questions.

Did You Know?

Posting your résumé online with a major job site is not going to be good enough. On average about a half-million résumés are posted on top job sites each and every week. The best way to step to the front of the job opening line is to get in front of the employer, in person.

Fill Out an Application

YOU WILL NEED:
- Blank job application
- Black or blue ballpoint pen
- Professional and personal references
- At least one form of state or federal identification

TIME REQUIRED:
- 30–45 minutes

Seldom will you get a second chance to make a first impression, and your application is just that—a first impression. Applications give a potential employer a glance at who you are and what you have done. So being neat, complete, and professional is always a good way to start.

STEP 1 **Target the market.**

You're going to put in some legwork to find a job, so before you do, try a little preplanning to save time—and gas money—before you hit the streets. See STEPS 1 and 2 in "How to Interview for a Job."

STEP 2 **Dress to impress.**

When you are gathering job applications, be sure to dress well. You may actually find yourself speaking to the hiring manager or even be asked to interview immediately. (See "How to Interview for a Job")

STEP 3 **Read all instructions.**

Be sure to carefully read all of the instructions before you begin filling anything out to ensure that you understand the application questions.

STEP 4 **Fill out the application.**

Use a ballpoint pen to neatly and honestly complete the application. Detail your prior work history in the specified location on the application. You will be asked to provide two or three references. Describe your relationship and provide contact information for each reference. (See "How to Ask for a Reference")

STEP 5 **Include supplementary documents.**

To verify your identity, the employer may ask to photocopy your driver's license or a state or federally issued ID.

STEP 6 **Proofread.**

Make a good impression on the hiring manager by being sure your application is error-free.

STEP 7 **Turn in the application.**

Similar to when you picked up the application, dress appropriately in the event that you speak with the manager or are invited to interview for the position.

Man Fact or Fiction:

Spelling and grammar don't count on an application if the job involves physical labor.

Fiction. The fact is, a few spelling errors probably won't get your application tossed in the round file (trash can), but more than a few will. When in doubt, spell-check before filling in the blanks on an application.

Interview
for a Job

YOU WILL NEED:
- Work résumé
- List of references
- Letters of recommendation
- Interview-appropriate clothing
- List of questions
- Thank-you note

TIME REQUIRED:
- Varies, 10–30 minutes

You made it in the door. Congratulations. Now that you are face-to-face with your potential boss, you'll need to nail the interview. So dress to impress, use your manners, and remember this time is valuable, so come prepared and you could leave employed.

STEP 1 **Analyze yourself.**

Determine what type of job you are interested in performing. Outline your skills and qualifications.

STEP 2 **Find an opening.**

Search for a job opening that matches your interests, skills, and qualifications.

STEP 3 **Research the company.**

Gather information on the company's goals, work standards, and job qualifications to determine if you are a good fit for the work environment.

STEP 4 **Prepare yourself.**

Practice interviewing to ensure you are confident when it comes time to interview. Organize a professional portfolio that includes a copy of your résumé, list of references, and at least one letter of recommendation.

STEP 5 **Dress to impress.**

Choose interview-appropriate clothes. Dress to or slightly above the professional standards of the company. Do not wear your favorite/lucky T-shirt, sagging pants, hat, hoodie, earphones, cologne, chain tethering your wallet to your belt, or "gold" necklace on the outside of your shirt.

STEP 6 **Stay focused.**

During your interview, listen carefully and answer clearly the interviewer's questions. Do not add unnecessary details to your answers.

STEP 7 **Ask good questions.**

Be prepared to ask your interviewer any professional question you need answered about the job, scheduled hours required to work, and performance expectations.

STEP 8 **Follow up.**

After your interview, send a thank-you note to the interviewer. This is your opportunity to remind them of your qualifications and what makes you a good fit for the job.

Wise Guy

"It's not that you need to wear a suit; however, you do need to dress appropriate for the interview position. Your body piercings or tattoos don't need to show, yet your self-confidence, willingness to learn, and pride in a job well done does."

—Gino Quintana,
guest services manager,
Hilton Hotels & Resorts,
Hilton Houston North

Ask for a Raise

YOU WILL NEED:

- Current pay research
- List of your accomplishments that warrant a raise

TIME REQUIRED:

- 30 minutes

So, you're thinking it's time you get a raise. Well, get in line, the long line. Nearly half of all workers believe they too are worth more, yet few do anything proactive to increase their pay. Most employees wait for the company to give out raises and feel undervalued when the boss doesn't. The best way to up your pay is to move from the long "waiting" line into the short "asking" line. If you are reasonable, reliable, hardworking, and have been on the job for more than a few months, it may be time to ask for a raise. Remember, those who don't ask, don't get.

STEP 1 **Do your research.**

Determine how much others in your same position are earning.

STEP 2 **Assess the workplace atmosphere.**

Do your best to determine if this is an appropriate time for the company to increase your pay.

STEP 3 **Schedule a meeting.**

When asking your boss for a raise, you should ask in person. Never through a call, a text, or an email.

STEP 4 **Prepare for your meeting.**

Outline your accomplishments and confidently list the reasons why the quality of your job performance is worth more than you are currently making.

STEP 5 **Meet with your boss.**

In person, clearly present your request to your boss. Be prepared for whatever decision they make.

Did You Know?

Employers are required to pay their employees a minimum wage that meets or exceeds federal laws. Yet, some states allow employers to include money received from service tips in an employee's minimum wage calculation. When asking for a raise in the service industry, be sure to clarify how a raise will impact your hourly wage and tip totals.

Ask for a Promotion

YOU WILL NEED:

- Proven record of success in your current position
- Open position in the company
- Clear understanding of your professional strengths

TIME REQUIRED:

- 15 minutes

Want to know the best way to get promoted? It's no big rocket science secret (unless you work for NASA). By definition a promotion is an upgrade, an advancement, or an elevated position. So the best way to work your way up to a promotion is to raise the bar on yourself. This means committing to do your very best in the job you already have. Once you are doing your work to near-perfect performance, your boss may see that you are ready to step up to the next challenge.

STEP 1 Consider the atmosphere.

If the company is going through a period of layoffs, this may not be an appropriate time to approach your boss for a promotion.

STEP 2 Determine the need.

If there is a job opening, you can apply for the job. If there is not an open position, determine the need of the company and how you are able to meet the need.

STEP 3 Evaluate your strengths.

Highlight your contributions to the company and be prepared to present them to your boss.

STEP 4 Approach your boss.

Schedule a face-to-face meeting with your boss to discuss your potential for a promotion.

STEP 5 Be specific.

Outline a need in the company and how you can best fill that need. Anticipate questions from your boss and be prepared to defend your request.

STEP 6 Wait for a decision.

Do not pressure your boss, but allow him or her time to come to a decision. Maintain a good attitude and work ethic regardless of the decision.

Wise Guy

"The secret to my success in business is that I learned to trust, like, and respect the customer."

—Peter Georgescu

Mr. Georgescu was abducted as a child and put to work in a forced labor camp in Romania. After eight years of separation, he was reunited with his parents in America, where he started school, learned English, and worked hard to respect and gain the respect of others. In time, he rose to become CEO of a multinational communications company.

Resign

YOU WILL NEED:
- Letter of resignation

TIME REQUIRED:
- Minimum 2 weeks

> Your work is going to fill a large part of your life, and the only way to be truly satisfied is to do what you believe is great work. And the only way to do great work is to love what you do. If you haven't found it yet, keep looking. Don't settle. As with all matters of the heart, you'll know when you find it.
>
> —Steve Jobs

STEP 1 **Put it in writing.**

Create a short professional letter of resignation. This letter should be clear, be free from personal emotions, indicate a specific departure date, outline your achievements, and express gratitude to your boss and the company.

STEP 2 **Edit your letter.**

Be sure your letter is free from all spelling and grammar errors.

STEP 3 **Turn in your letter.**

At least two weeks prior to your resignation date, personally present your letter of resignation to your boss and the human resources department. Keep a copy of the letter for your personal records.

STEP 4 **Ask for a recommendation.**

If appropriate, ask your boss for a personal recommendation that you can use in the future.

STEP 5 **Work to replace yourself.**

Aid in the process of finding your replacement and training them before you leave.

STEP 6 **Check into benefits.**

You may be entitled to benefits from the company upon your departure. Check with the human resources department to see if this is the case.

STEP 7 **Return company property.**

Prior to your departure, return all company-owned items to the appropriate departments. This will help to ensure that you leave on good terms.

Wise Guy

"Always end on a good note. Don't think of your last day on the job as your opportunity to tell people what you really think about them or the job. You never know when you might find yourself working with, or for, them again."

—Jim Agnew, CTE instructor,
Bellevue School District, Bellevue, WA

Ask for a Reference

Possible References

- Mr. Agnew, teacher
- Mrs. Harrell, family friend
- Mr. Martin, previous boss
- Mr. Toles, mentor

YOU WILL NEED:

- List of respectable people familiar with your performance
- Email addresses
- Phone numbers

TIME REQUIRED:

- 30 minutes

Some surprises are good and some are not. One surprise you should never force on a person is to use them as a reference without their permission. "*Awkward.*" Any boss, co-worker, teacher, or friend needs to be asked before you list them as a reference. This way you will be directing potential employers toward positive references and away from anybody negative.

STEP 1 Create a list.

Write down a list of people who will give honest feedback about your past performance.

STEP 2 Consider email.

Sending an email first can be the best way to request a reference because it doesn't put the receiver on the spot. If they agree to recommend you, good. If not, they can decline without the awkwardness of telling you no in person.

STEP 3 Draft an email.

Write a simple straight-to-the-point message about the role you are seeking and your request for their recommendation. Do not ask, "Can you give me a reference?" Do ask something like, "Do you feel comfortable giving me a good reference?" Be sure to briefly answer these key questions: What is the role you are seeking? Why is this role important to you? When do you need to hear back with a yes or no about your reference request?

STEP 4 Proofread your request.

Have somebody else proofread your reference request. Pick a proofreader who will tell you what you need to know about your writing skills and not simply what you want to hear.

STEP 5 Send the email.

Send each reference request individually. Do not send out a group email. Briefly personalize each request with something the reader will value about your relationship.

STEP 6 Follow up.

When you hear back about your request, follow up with another email or, better yet, a phone call. Despite their answer of yes or no, thank the person for their thoughtful consideration.

Man Fact or Fiction:
Men send thank-you notes.

Fact. Americans spend between $7 billion and $8 billion on greeting cards each year. Second only to birthday cards, thank-you cards are given to millions of appreciated people each year.

WEALTH & MONEY MANAGEMENT

4

According to the Bureau of Engraving and Printing, the average dollar bill stays in circulation a mere 21 months. Right around the paperback's second birthday, most are retired due to excessive wear. In his short lifespan, "George" experiences thousands of spending sprees as he trades hands an estimated 10,000 times. Seldom does he meet an owner willing to keep him more than a few days, let alone one who values investing in a long-term relationship. Unable to deny the temporary satisfaction of an impulsive buy, most guys spend their every dollar on "wants" rather than saving like men for true "needs." A mature man knows, the larger his collection of George Washington portraits grows, the quicker they will unite and change their name to Benjamin Franklin.

One of today's top money-management experts is Benjamin-collecting, straight-talking author, TV and radio host Dave Ramsey. With energy to spare and a direct way with words, Mr. Ramsey makes no excuse for being bold and blunt about how people need to think and act differently with their money. His money makeover insights are invaluable for any man wanting to master his money and escape the grasp of slavery to debt.

Mr. Ramsey speaks from experience when he shares his advice about spending, saving, and the danger of drowning in debt. His "been there, done that" life experience includes fighting his way free from the enslavement of debt. Now a financial freedom fighter, he shares the knowledge he gained about first managing himself and then his money differently to assist others in breaking their bond to the almighty dollar:

> After losing everything, I went on a quest to find out how money really works, how I could get control of it and how I could have confidence in handling it. I read everything I could get my hands on. I interviewed older rich people, people who made money and kept it. That quest led me to a really, really uncomfortable place: my mirror. I came to realize that my money problems, worries and shortages largely began and ended with the person in my mirror. I also realized that if I could learn to manage the character I shaved with every morning, I would win with money.[1]

For more than 20 years now, Dave Ramsey has counseled millions of people with the same financial strategies he used to master his money.

Here is a small sampling of people's favorite Dave Ramsey commonsense sayings and wisdom about managing money and life:

"We buy things we don't need with money we don't have in order to impress people we don't like."[2]

"I believe that through knowledge and discipline, financial peace is possible for all of us."[3]

"You must gain control over your money or the lack of it will forever control you."[4]

"If you will live like no one else, later you can live like no one else."[5]

"You've got to tell your money what to do or it will leave."[6]

"You can't be in debt and win. It doesn't work."[7]

"Work is a surefire money-making scheme."[8]

"Act your wage."[9]

Act your wage? Sounds funny, yet any wealthy man knows these three words are the fastest way to financial freedom. Still, you are probably thinking it would be nice to act like a millionaire. Who wouldn't? According to Mr. Ramsey, the trick to retiring as a millionaire is a matter of choice. "Did you know $100 a month invested from age 30 to age 70, just $100 a month, latte breath, pizza boy, do I need to go further about golf? No, I won't get personal and insult anybody. But just $100 a month from age 30 to age 70 invested in a decent growth stock mutual fund in your Roth IRA, tax-free, would be about $1,176,000. There is no excuse for you to not retire a millionaire."[10]

A hundred bucks a month? Yep, just $100 a month. That may sound like a lot right now; yet think about how much cash most guys toss without knowing where it went. What did you buy in the past month? Now consider where you want to be in your financial future. Millionaire or not, learning how to master your money will keep it from becoming the master of you.

Meet Dave Ramsey

David L. Ramsey III is married, the father of three, a financial author, radio host, television personality, motivational speaker, and business owner who has an estimated net worth of $55 million.

Create a Personal Budget

YOU WILL NEED:
- Lined paper
- Sharp pencil
- Calculator

TIME REQUIRED:
- 30 minutes

Remember when that guy in class complained, "This math is stupid. When will I ever use this stuff?" The truthful answer is simple: every day. Your first step on the path to financial freedom is using some basic math to create a personal budget. Knowing how to add and subtract gives a guy the power to determine if he is spending more or less than he makes. A mature man adds value in his life by creating a purposeful budget that directs him to financial freedom. An immature guy subtracts value from his life by losing his way in debt and financial slavery. To quote John Maxwell, "A budget is telling your money where to go instead of wondering where it went."[11]

STEP 1 **Determine your income.**

List all the consistent ways you make money each month.

STEP 2 **Total your income.**

Add up the money earned and subtract any taxes you must pay. This is your total monthly income.

STEP 3 **List your expenses.**

Where do you spend your money each month? List everything. Yes, everything! Categorize if needed, but every penny spent must be accounted for!

STEP 4 **Identify your fixed expenses.**

Review your list of expenses for things you can't live without. Fixed expenses are things you are committed to each month, month after month. Expenses like rent, utilities, insurance, and food should top this list.

STEP 5 **Total your monthly fixed expenses.**

Add up your fixed expenses and this is your total monthly fixed expense budget.

STEP 6 **Do the math.**

Subtract your fixed expenses from your income. If you have money left over, congratulations. Your budget is "in the black" because you are living "below your means." You can move to STEP 9. If you are out of cash, your budget is "in the red." You are living "above your means" and need to either increase your income or reduce your expenses.

STEP 7 **Identify your flexible expenses.**

Review your original expenses list for expenditures you can live without.

STEP 8 **Total your monthly flexible expenses.**

If you are spending "above your means," you'll need to reduce your flexible expenses (or increase your income) to get to your goal of being "in the black."

Watch your money.

Keep an account of all your expenses. Cash, debit, and credit transactions need to be recorded and reviewed each month. This will help you stay accountable to where and why your money is being spent.

More Info

Have you included charitable giving in your monthly budget? Many financially savvy men give 10% of their income away each month. Start with what you know you can afford, and increase it as your budget and compassion allows.

Build a Savings Account

YOU WILL NEED:

- Income
- Savings account at a bank
- Personal budget
- Willpower

TIME REQUIRED:

- 1+ years

> Save a part of your income and begin now, for the man with a surplus controls circumstances and the man without a surplus is controlled by circumstances.
>
> —Henry Buckley

STEP 1 **Create a personal budget.**

See "How to Create a Personal Budget."

STEP 2 **Set a financial goal.**

Identify how much you want to save and by when you want it saved. This will require you to revisit your personal budget and make the changes needed to reprioritize some of your flexible spending as savings.

STEP 3 **Pay off debt.**

If you owe others money, be sure to put first things first by paying off debt. Use the money you reprioritized in your budget for savings to pay back any debts. Not only will you be free from the burden of owing, but you will also be released from the additional expense of the debt's interest rate.

STEP 4 **Open a savings account.**

Take your first deposit to a reputable bank and open an interest-bearing savings account. *Interest-bearing* means the bank will pay you a set percentage of your account balance just for keeping your money in their bank. It's not much, but your money will grow over time.

STEP 5 **Keep to your budget.**

Now that you have included saving in your monthly budget, be sure to contribute to your savings account as planned before giving in to the temptation of an impulse purchase.

STEP 6 **Stay out of debt.**

Why buy when you can't afford it? If a purchase is not part of your budget, don't buy it. With the single swipe of a card or stroke of a pen, you can kill your savings.

STEP 7 **Repeat STEPS 5–7.**

Wise Guy

"The art is not in making money, but in keeping it."

—Proverb

Manage a Credit Card Account

YOU WILL NEED:
- Income
- Credit card
- Personal budget
- Willpower

TIME REQUIRED:
- 15 minutes per month

American consumers owe more than $850 billion in credit card debt. That's a lot of money owed and even more that will be paid once interest rates are calculated and collected. Properly managing a credit card keeps you from paying more than you owe. Owing money to a credit card company is like being enslaved to debt. The key to avoiding the bondage of debt is to not spend what you don't have. Despite how much you want to buy something, think of how much you don't want to be bound to debt. Think of it this way: The fun of building up debt is short lived, while the pain of tearing it back down again can last a lifetime.

STEP 1 **Limit your choices.**

You do not need more than one credit card.

STEP 2 **Know your credit card's terms and conditions.**

This includes your maximum credit line, interest rate, payment due date, and any transaction fees specific to your card.

STEP 3 **Charge only if you must.**

Your credit card should be a last resort payment option. Use it for emergencies when cash or debit payments are not an option. Daily budgeted expenses should not be paid with a credit card whenever possible. (See "How to Create a Personal Budget")

STEP 4 **Review your monthly statements.**

Always look over the statement of purchases each month. Compare the statement to the accounting of your monthly budget. Keep an eye open for any unauthorized charges or fees, as they may be a sign of credit card fraud.

STEP 5 **Make your payments.**

Each month pay off your balance to avoid interest and service fees. Always pay before the due date to avoid late fees and any potential negative impact on your credit score.

Man Fact or Fiction:
The first credit card was made out of leather.

Fiction. The fact is, the first credit card was most likely paper. Since then, credit cards or credit tokens have been made from metal coins, metal plates, fiber, paper, and plastic, but not leather.

Invest in the Future

YOU WILL NEED:

- Income
- Long-term investment account
- Patience

TIME REQUIRED:

- 30 minutes a month for the next 40+ years

Many young guys don't believe investing in the future is very important. Most think they will have the rest of their life to save money, so why start now? The truth is, the earlier you start investing your hard-earned money, the more money you will have when you want to stop working so hard.

STEP 1 **Begin with the end in mind.**

Think ahead to when you want to stop working. Most people set their sights on age 65.

STEP 2 **Earn an income.**

To invest money for tomorrow you need to earn money today. So get a job and set aside a percentage of your pay for investment.

STEP 3 **Pick an investment plan.**

Ask trusted adults to recommend a financial advisor who can guide you to a long-term investment plan that takes advantage of compound interest.

STEP 4 **Start early.**

The key to maximizing your money is to start investing as soon as possible. Here's what will happen to an investment earning 10% that is compounded yearly:

$10,000 invested at age 20 will be $728,905 by age 65
$10,000 invested at age 25 will be $452,593 by age 65
$10,000 invested at age 30 will be $281,024 by age 65
$10,000 invested at age 40 will be $108,347 by age 65

Wise Guy

"Financial peace isn't the acquisition of stuff. It's learning to live on less than you make, so you can give money back and have money to invest. You can't win until you do this."[12]

—Dave Ramsey

Live Debt-Free

YOU WILL NEED:
- Income
- Self-control
- Patience

TIME REQUIRED:
- From now on

Few truer words have been spoken about living debt-free than those shared by the eighteenth-century Scottish moral philosopher and political economist Adam Smith: "What can be added to the happiness of the man who is in health, who is out of debt, and has a clear conscience?"[13] The value that comes with living debt free has been compared with being freed from the chains of slavery. Mr. Smith lived in a time when one man could own another man; and he opposed the act—whether it was physical or financial. Debt is slavery and freedom is life. So take Adam Smith's advice and stay free, my friend.

STEP 1 Earn an income.

Financial independence begins when you earn your own income.

STEP 2 Value your money.

Money is a tool, not a toy. You work hard to earn it, so look for ways to make your money work hard for you.

STEP 3 Know your needs.

Be realistic about what you really need versus what you want to buy. Having enough to buy what you need should never be at the mercy of throwing money at your wants.

STEP 4 Create a personal budget.

Telling your money where to go beats wondering where it went. (See "How to Create a Personal Budget")

STEP 5 Pay cash.

It hurts to pay cash for stuff, so you won't want to part with your money so easily. You can also bargain better when flashing the Benjamins.

STEP 6 Save.

Work your budget with the goal of your income being greater than your expenses. Deposit the remaining money into your savings and long-term investment accounts.

STEP 7 Don't spend what you don't have.

Stay away from buying and carrying a balance on a credit card. (See "How to Manage a Credit Card Account")

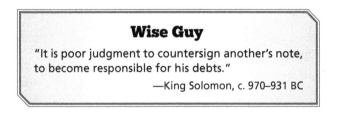

Wise Guy

"It is poor judgment to countersign another's note, to become responsible for his debts."

—King Solomon, c. 970–931 BC

GROOMING & PERSONAL HYGIENE

5

From the top of his head to the bottom of his feet, man is made up of more than 5,000 individual parts. Not knowing how all those parts work together only adds to the confusion many guys feel about doing life within their own skin.

Most people don't think much about properly caring for their health. Yet those who do, tend to look better, feel better, and live better lives. The vast majority of a guy's attention is often on what the mirror reflects about his outward health—thinking that if he looks good enough on the outside there is no need to consider the team effort happening within. But the truth is, every man's body is a complex build of bones, muscles, organs, nerves, hormones, and hundreds of odd parts that can only be identified by doctors in white lab coats.

One of the world's top docs is a man who thinks about all the odd inner parts and how each works together to influence our overall health. Dr. Thomas R. Frieden is the director of the US Centers for Disease Control and Prevention, and he has a strong grasp on what health issues men need to consider early on, before it's too late. At the top of his list for men is heart health. You think heart disease is for old dudes? Wrong, says Dr. Frieden. The top three factors that turn a guy's ticker into a time bomb are smoking, high blood pressure, and lack of exercise. Healthy men put controls on each before they're controlled by them.

1. Don't smoke. The Centers for Disease Control and Prevention emphasizes that young men are underestimating the health risks associated with smoking and overestimating their ability to quit the habit. Forty percent of young smokers have unsuccessfully tried to quit their addiction to nicotine. This is bad news considering cigarettes contain at least 60 substances known to cause cancer. Each year cigarette smoke is responsible for one-third of all cancer deaths. This only contributes to the more than 430,000 people who die yearly from smoking-related disease. "If you smoke, quitting is by far the single most important thing you can do to improve your own health," said Dr. Frieden in a 2013 Google+ chat with the editor-in-chief of *Men's Health* magazine.

2. Lower your blood pressure. A healthy man's blood pressure should read 120 over 80 (120/80). The number 120 is the measurement of pressure placed on the walls of your arteries when your heart beats. The 80 represents the pressure between beats. High blood pressure is no longer just the curse of overweight old men. Elevated blood pressure is on the rise in young men also. The biggest reasons many guys are headed for heart disease are an inactive lifestyle, an unhealthy diet, and apathy about obesity. Heart health is a decision men need to make while they're young. Here are a few ways you can beat the odds and keep your blood pressure low:

Eat healthy. This means less salt and more fruits and veggies.

Sleep. Getting less than 7 to 8 hours of sleep a night can impact your body's ability to regulate stress hormones, leading to high blood pressure.

Exercise. Movement works not only the muscles you can see flexing but also the one that flexes 24/7: your heart.

3. Exercise daily. Dr. Frieden practices what he teaches. A dedicated squash player, he leaves his sweat on the court and takes a healthy heart with him everywhere he goes. His advice for you is this: "Physical activity really is the closest thing we have to a wonder drug. Even if you don't lose an ounce of weight, it will help you control your blood pressure, not have diabetes, be less likely to have cancer, improve your mood, and reduce your cholesterol. It really has a tremendous number of positive effects. So the challenge really is to get started and keep it up."[1]

There is no question that living in your own skin can be a confusing existence. Staying healthy is a learned skill and perhaps one of the best ways to show others you are a man in control of your life, from the inside out.

Meet Dr. Thomas R. Frieden

Tom Frieden, MD, MPH, is the director of the Centers for Disease Control and Prevention (CDC). Dr. Frieden has worked to control health threats from infectious diseases, respond to emergencies, and battle the leading causes of suffering and death in the United States and around the world. He has received many awards and honors, and has published more than 200 scientific articles.

Shave

YOU WILL NEED:
- Shaving cream or gel
- New razor
- Clean washcloth
- Sink
- Facial stubble

TIME REQUIRED:
- 5 minutes

To shave, or not to shave: that is the question. If your face is an uneven sprouting of peach fuzz, bald spots, chin weed, and that one long cat-like whisker, then *yes*, it's time to start shaving. Yet if your face is still follicly-challenged, don't worry. Your time to master the skill of dragging laser-cut steel over tender cheeks will arrive soon enough. Just remember, stubble doesn't make you a man. The answer to what separates the boys from men in the facial scruff category has less to do with if you can grow it and more to do with if you can shave it without nicking and slicing your face to shreds.

STEP 1 **Fill the sink.**

Run warm water into the clean sink until it's filled halfway.

STEP 2 **Wet your face.**

Using a warm washcloth, wet your face for about a minute to soften your facial hair.

STEP 3 **Apply shaving cream.**

Squirt a golf-ball-sized amount of shaving cream into the palm of your hand. With your other hand, dab and apply a thin, even layer over the area you will shave.

STEP 4 **Shave.**

Applying light but firm pressure with the razor, shave in the same direction that your whiskers grow. Start at the base of your sideburns and shave downward to your jawline using long, even strokes.

STEP 5 **Rinse your razor.**

Use the warm water in the sink to rinse your razor after a few strokes. This keeps the space between the blades from clogging with hair.

STEP 6 **Shave the area around your chin.**

Pull the razor downward from your chin toward your neck or upward from your neck toward your chin, depending on which direction is most comfortable and effective. Raise your chin up and tilt your head back to tighten the skin for a closer shave.

STEP 7 **Shave your upper lip.**

Keep the skin on your upper lip tight by curling your lip down over your top teeth. Shave down from your nose to your lip.

STEP 8 **Shave your lower lip.**

Keep the skin on your lower lip tight by curling your lip up over your bottom teeth. Shave down from your lip to your chin.

STEP 9 **Check your work.**

Wash away any excess shaving cream and examine your face for hairs that remain unshaved. Check the edge of your jawline, in front of your ears, near your lips, and nostrils. Carefully re-shave any hairs you missed.

STEP 10 **Wash away excess shaving cream.**

With a wet washcloth, wipe your face clean. Reexamine your face for nicks that may bleed slightly. If you are nicked, don't freak out. You won't bleed out, and you'll bear no permanent scars. Simply apply a small piece of tissue to the nick. This will help stop the bleeding. Just remember to remove the tissue before leaving the house.

BONUS STEP

Apply cold water or aftershave to your face to avoid razor burn. If your face feels on fire after you shave, see "How to Cool Razor Burn."

Man Fact or Fiction:
Shaving makes hair grow back thicker and faster.

Fiction. The fact is, shaving doesn't affect hair growth or thickness. Hair may appear to be thicker simply because cut ends are blunt and more obvious.

Cool Razor Burn

YOU WILL NEED:
- Clean washcloth
- Cold water
- Aloe Vera aftershave gel

TIME REQUIRED:
- 3 minutes

Ouch! It burns. It itches. Red bumps are rising on your face! No matter how you cut it, razor burn is not cool. The good news is, the red rash can be effectively evaded. Before your next shave, make sure you ditch the cheap shaving cream for a quality gel, use a new sharp, multiblade razor, and please resist the urge to scrape those hard blades over your soft skin with so much pressure. When you do experience the heat of razor burn, try these simple steps to douse the facial flames.

STEP 1 **Do not scratch your face.**

This may further irritate your skin and even cause an infection.

STEP 2 **Wet your face.**

Wet a fresh, clean washcloth with cold water. Apply the cool cloth to the irritated skin of your face. This will restrict the blood flow to the small capillaries in the surface layers of your skin and reduce the visible redness.

STEP 3 **Do not scrub your face with the cloth.**

This may also further irritate your skin and even cause an infection.

STEP 4 **Do not apply aftershave or cologne.**

These products may contain alcohol and can irritate your skin even more. Like tossing fuel on a fire, the alcohol in aftershave and cologne will only make your facial flames feel hotter!

STEP 5 **Soothe the skin.**

Apply a fragrance-free aloe vera gel or an all-natural emollient cream. Use about a quarter-sized amount of nature's herbal remedy and your face will thank you.

Did You Know?

Facial hair grows about ½ inch a month, which measures out to about 6 inches a year. The clean-shaven man will spend an average of more than 3,000 hours of his life shaving.

How To

Apply Deodorant or Antiperspirant

YOU WILL NEED:
- Stick antiperspirant or deodorant
- Clean, dry armpits

TIME REQUIRED:
- 15 seconds

Applying stick antiperspirant or deodorant isn't difficult. What is difficult is sitting next to the guy who forgets to wear the stuff. Think of it this way. The smell of pungent pits is one of the most powerful female repellants known to humankind. Close behind on the nasty scale is when your arm goes up and a wet pit stain shouts out, "I'm sweaty!" Living with that kind of embarrassment, now that's difficult. But don't sweat it. There is a simple solution. Wear antiperspirant or deodorant—or a combination of both.

STEP 1 **Remove the cap.**

Peel off any product seal from the stick of antiperspirant or deodorant.

STEP 2 **Raise one arm.**

Lift your arm over your head to expose your open, dry armpit.

STEP 3 **Apply the deodorant.**

Swiping up and down in even strokes, apply the deodorant to the skin of your armpit. Repeat under your other arm. Two or three strokes should ensure complete coverage. Too much and people will smell your deodorant before they can see you.

STEP 4 **Dry time.**

Before putting on a shirt, allow a minute for the deodorant to dry so it won't leave a visible mark on your clothing.

In the Pits: Antiperspirants vs. Deodorants

Antiperspirants—According to the sweatperts at the University of North Carolina's Department of Dermatology, the key weapon used to combat underarm wetness is aluminum. Before you try rubbing a soda can under your arms, though, buy a stick of antiperspirant instead.

Antiperspirants help block sweat by introducing aluminum ions into the skin-level cells of the sweat glands in your armpit. When your glands begin to push water out, aluminum ions react with your perspiration, causing the cells to swell and squeezing the sweat ducts closed.

Deodorants—Classified as a cosmetic by the US Food and Drug Administration (FDA), deodorant is little more than an armpit air freshener formulated to mask the foul-smelling body odor all humans emit. Yep, everybody has a unique "odortype." Your odortype is a mix of environmental factors, including when you showered last, if you used soap in that shower, what you eat, how much water you drink, and the DNA you inherited from your parents. There is no escaping the smell of your genetics, but you do control how often you shower and what you choose to chow. So keep both your body and food fresh for a better-smelling tomorrow.

Fight the smell of defeat by staying clean, eating right, and wearing a combination of antiperspirant and deodorant that works for you. It may take you a few tries to find the right brand, but don't give up. Noses everywhere will thank you.

Apply Hair-Styling Product

YOU WILL NEED:
- Clean, washed hair
- Hair product
  (pomade for a slight shine,
  wax for the matted look)

TIME REQUIRED:
- 1 minute

> Life is an endless struggle full of
> frustrations and challenges, but eventually
> you find a hair stylist you like.
>
> —Author Unknown

STEP 1 **Towel dry hair.**

This allows the styling product to become evenly distributed in your hair. When hair is too wet, the product can't cling to the hair. Too dry and the product will clump.

STEP 2 **Select your product.**

Choose a pomade if you want your hair to hold a slight shine. Use a wax product when the matted look is more your style. Place a dime-sized amount of styling product in your palm.

STEP 3 **Work the product.**

Rub your palms together, working the product until it's evenly spread across the palm sides of both hands.

STEP 4 **Apply product.**

Use your fingers to work the product into your hair. Start at the crown of your head and work forward. Be sure to apply the product down to the base of your hair next to the scalp.

STEP 5 **Style hair.**

Use your fingers, a comb, or a brush to style hair to your desired look.

Wise Guy

"Two important things to remember if you care about your hair. First, get to know your barber or stylist. Find one you like and insist that only they cut your hair. Second, it doesn't matter if you go to a walk-in chop shop or guy-friendly salon; don't go cheap with your hair. When it comes to shampoo, styling products, and haircuts, you get what you pay for. Spending a few extra bucks once a month is worth it. There is no comparison between a good haircut, even on a bad hair day, and a bad haircut with three bad-hair weeks to go before it grows out."

—Hudson, celebrity stylist
and owner of Hudson E. Hudson Salon

Wear Cologne

YOU WILL NEED:
- Bottle of carefully chosen cologne
- Clean, dry neck

TIME REQUIRED:
- 30 seconds

Apply too much cologne and people will smell you before they see you. This is not good. You want those who get close enough to notice your cologne to think, "Yeah, he smells nice." Which is much better than, "Yuck! Did he take a bath in that stuff?" When it comes to wearing cologne, bolder is not better.

STEP 1 **Wear one scent.**

Make sure you are not wearing any other scented products. Aftershave, body wash, or deodorant with their own scent will only clash with the smell of your cologne. And no, the same brand-name products are not always intended to go together.

STEP 2 **Remove cap.**

Carefully open cologne spray or pour bottle.

STEP 3 **Apply cologne.**

At the base of your neck, apply a light amount of cologne to your skin. One or two drops or sprays should be all you need. Three is a potent, ABSOLUTE maximum!

IMPORTANT
Apply cologne only to your skin. The temperature of your skin interacts with the release of the scent in your cologne. Don't apply to your clothes. Cologne can stain fabric and the smell can change depending on the laundry products used to clean your clothes.

STEP 4 **Recap cologne.**

You don't want to spill this stuff.

SUGGESTION
Don't wear cologne every day. And try a new scent every few months.

Did You Know?

Many counterfeit colognes use ingredients not certified by the FDA. The imposter product can produce an unattractive rash on your skin or even a health-threatening allergic reaction. True, your girlfriend might not sniff out the knockoff cologne. But your skin may not hide your guilt. So keep it real.

Freshen Bad Breath

YOU WILL NEED:
- Toothbrush and toothpaste
- Floss
- Drinking water
- Sugar-free cinnamon gum

TIME REQUIRED:
- 5 minutes

Halitosis. Say it out loud. Hal-i-to-sis. Did you hear yourself put emphasis on the "toe" in halitosis? Probably. Well, despite how the word is correctly pronounced, halitosis is not a foot fungus lurking on a dirty locker room floor. Halitosis is the fancy scientific name for the common condition known the world round as bad breath. So how do you keep your mouth from smelling like your feet? Simple, just follow a few fresh steps to a cleaner mouth.

STEP 1 **Brush your teeth.**

Get in the habit of brushing your pearly whites at least twice a day. Give them a cleaning for two minutes. One minute on your uppers and one minute on your lowers.

STEP 2 **Clean your tongue.**

Stick out your tongue and look in the mirror. What color is it? If it isn't a clean, fleshy pink color, use your toothbrush to scrape the surface clean. Be careful not to gag yourself. Puke breath is nasty.

STEP 3 **Floss.**

You will be surprised how much food jams down between your chompers. After flossing, smell the floss. Seriously. If your floss stinks like a Porta-Potty, it's because bacteria are depositing their "deposits" along your gum line. These microscopic-sized "number twos" cause gum disease, and that gum disease stinks. No brand of trendy gum can fix that kind of dirty mouth. So what's the solution? Floss. Every day. Your mouth and your floss should smell better in about a week. If they don't, talk with your dentist—from a safe distance please.

STEP 4 **Drink more water.**

"But I don't like the taste of water," some guys say. Well, man up! Water keeps your mouth hydrated and helps produce saliva. Saliva is bacteria's worst enemy because it contains germ-slaying antiseptic and enzymes. Less bacteria in your mouth means less of their "waste" is deposited between your teeth. Their digested waste is just like your digested waste. It stinks. So help flush it away by drinking water.

STEP 5 **Chew sugar-free gum.**

Chewing gum encourages the production of saliva. But stay away from the super-sugary gums. Bacteria thrive on sugar. Try cinnamon-flavored gum because cinnamon also reduces bacteria reproduction in the mouth. That and it smells good.

STEP 6 **Eat healthy.**

Two types of food can really make your breath reek. Smelly food like garlic, onions, cheese, and coffee pack a pungent punch. You will also want to cut out junk foods high in sugar and fat. Bacteria thrive on sugar and fat.

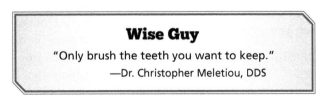

Wise Guy
"Only brush the teeth you want to keep."
—Dr. Christopher Meletiou, DDS

Wash Your Hands Properly

:20–:30

YOU WILL NEED:
- Running water (warm or cold)
- Soap
- Clean towel

TIME REQUIRED:
- 1 minute

Guys grab some seriously dirty stuff every day without thinking about it. Curious minds at the Wright-Patterson Medical Center in Dayton, Ohio, did the research and discovered these filthy facts. The #1 germ-ridden thing we handle is an average $1 bill. Additional top touches on the disgusting list include light switches, keyboards, cell phones, and toilet seats. Sound familiar? Avoiding these contaminated conveniences is next to impossible, yet there is one highly effective way guys can keep clean. Wash your hands. Regularly.

STEP 1 **Wet hands.**

Under clean running water, wet your hands up to your wrists.

STEP 2 **Apply soap.**

Bar or liquid soap will do.

STEP 3 **Lather hands.**

Vigorously rub your hands together to create soap lather from your fingertips to wrists.

STEP 4 **Scrub hands.**

For at least 20 seconds, scrub the back of your hands, between your fingers, and under your nails.

STEP 5 **Rinse hands.**

Under running water, rinse the soap lather from your hands.

STEP 6 **Dry hands.**

Use a clean towel or air to dry your hands.

STEP 7 **Turn off water.**

If possible, use your drying towel to turn water off.

More Info

Knowing when to wash is key to maintaining good health:

Before—food preparation, eating, brushing your teeth, caring for a sick friend, treating a wound, washing your face, unloading the dishwasher, holding a baby

After—food preparation, caring for a sick friend, treating a wound, using the bathroom, changing a diaper, blowing your nose, coughing, sneezing, feeding your pet, petting your pet, scooping your pet's mess, taking out the trash

Wash Your Face

YOU WILL NEED:
- Warm water
- Clean washcloth
- Face soap

TIME REQUIRED:
- 5 minutes

It's time to face the facts. Acne is the most common skin condition known to humankind. Teens seem to suffer more than most with 85% of all puberty-stricken guys affected by the condition. Call the "condition" what you like—acne, pimples, zits, blemishes, or puss pockets—guys worldwide are fighting to vanquish from their faces the invading whiteheads, blackheads, and the occasional chin volcano. So what can be done about it? Turns out, plenty, and it all starts with you learning how to properly wash your face.

STEP 1 Make it routine.

Clean your face and neck every morning, after any workout or physical activity that causes you to sweat, and each night before bed.

STEP 2 Wet a clean washcloth with warm water.

STEP 3 Hold the warm washcloth to your face and neck.

Repeat this application for about one minute. This will loosen surface dirt and open your skin pores.

STEP 4 Apply the mild soap to your face and neck.

Use a mild, nonirritating, and alcohol-free skin product. Apply on a soft washcloth and gently scrub your face, using a circular motion. Do not press too hard, as this could scuff the surface of your face, and do not scrub too vigorously, as this can irritate and dry out your skin. Dry skin is more likely to rash and increase oil production.

STEP 5 Rinse your face.

Use warm water to rinse all soap from your face and neck.

STEP 6 Don't touch!

Seriously. Your hands are covered with bacteria, and bacteria love to infest your face. "I don't touch my face!" you say. Really? Do you rest your elbow on your desk and your chin on your hand? Do you scratch, push, pick, or pinch at your pimples? Do you wash your hands often . . . like every hour? Yeah, that's what I thought. Now stop touching your face.

STEP 7 Eat and drink better.

What goes in must come out, and that includes through your skin. Your hormone balances react to your diet; and since acne is also linked to hormone imbalances, it's a good idea to watch what you eat. If you devour greasy foods high in saturated fats, salt, and sugar, your body responds by jacking up or turning down hormone balances. Skin is the body's largest organ, and it is supersensitive to your hormones. When you eat junk food, you can get junk skin. It's best to avoid deep-fried food, processed food, fast food, and energy drinks packed with ingredients difficult to pronounce. Your best practice is to drink less manufactured beverages and more of the natural stuff, aka water.

Man Fact or Fiction:
Tanning zaps zits.

Fiction. The fact is, UV rays from the sun or tanning beds damage your skin and can actually make acne blemishes worse.

Trim Your Fingernails

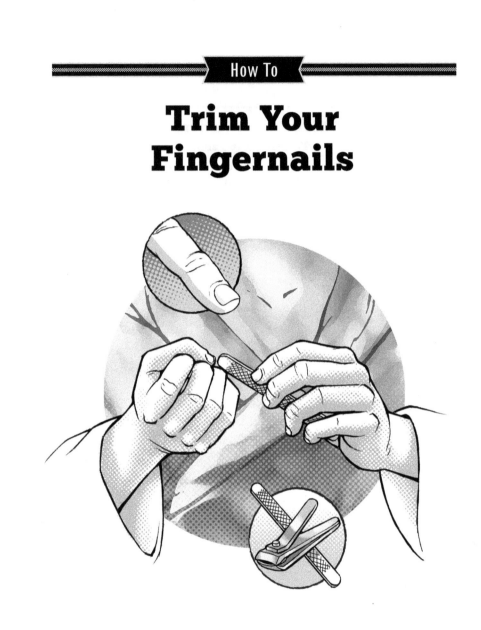

YOU WILL NEED:
- Sharp, clean nail cutter
- Nail file
- Wastebasket

TIME REQUIRED:
- 5 minutes

No biting! The space under your fingernails harbors double the count of germs and bacteria that is found on any other exposed place on your body. So don't nibble on your nails; trim them. You will be more socially acceptable, emotionally confident, and physically healthy.

STEP 1 **Soak your fingernails.**

In warm water, soak your fingernails before cutting. This finger bath softens the nails, making them easier to trim.

STEP 2 **Examine your nails.**

Keep an eye out for hangnails and any cuticle damage that may lead to an infection or nail damage.

STEP 3 **Cut your nails.**

Using a sharp, clean nail cutter, snip your nails straight across until they show a nice thin, even line of white at the end of the nail.

STEP 4 **File your nails.**

Once your nails have dried, use a nail file to smooth the edges. Uneven or jagged nails look sloppy and can catch on clothes, causing nails to tear or break.

STEP 5 **Final inspection.**

Give your nails a final inspection to ensure each is the same length and shape and nice-n-smooth. Clip and file each until all 10 nails look the same. When they do, you're done. Now repeat the same process on your toenails. Seriously . . . have you seen them lately?

Did You Know?

Fingernails grow faster than toenails and the nail of a man's index finger grows faster than his pinky fingernail.

Care for Your Feet

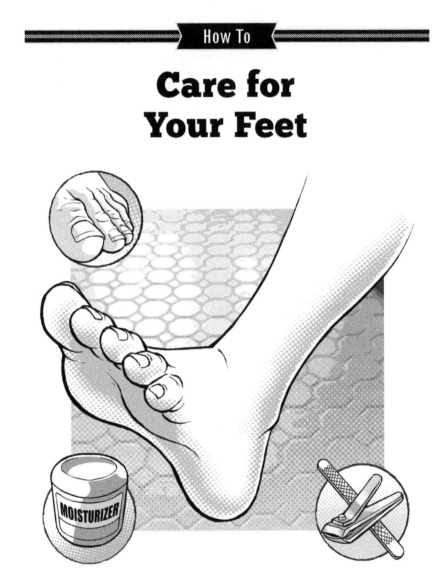

YOU WILL NEED:

- Soap, washcloth, towel
- Sharp, clean nail cutter
- Nail file
- Wastebasket
- Skin moisturizer

TIME REQUIRED:

- 10 minutes

Some guys fail to get a "foot up" in life because they don't bother to care for their feet. A good pair of walkers shouldn't send people running for the door when your shoes come off. Paying daily attention to your toes will stomp the stink and keep you standing tall next time you wear a pair of flip-flops.

STEP 1 ## Soak your feet.

Fill a tub with enough warm water to soak your feet.

STEP 2 ## Wash your feet.

Using soap and a washcloth, scrub your feet. Get down between each toe and under the nails. Dry each foot with a towel.

STEP 3 ## Examine your nails.

Look at each toe's nail, keeping an eye out for hangnails and any cuticle damage that could lead to an infection.

STEP 4 ## Cut your toenails.

Use a sharp, clean nail cutter to snip your nails so they show a nice thin, even line of white at the end of the nail. To avoid ingrown toenails, cut them nearly straight across instead of curved.

STEP 5 ## File your nails.

Once your nails are dry, use a nail file to smooth the edges. Uneven or jagged toenails look sloppy and can tear or break easily.

STEP 6 ## Moisturize.

Work the hand/foot skin moisturizer into your skin from the ankle down to your toes. Let the moisturizer absorb before putting on your socks.

Did You Know?

There are approximately 250,000 sweat glands in a pair of feet, and they excrete as much as half a pint of moisture each day.

CLOTHES & STYLE

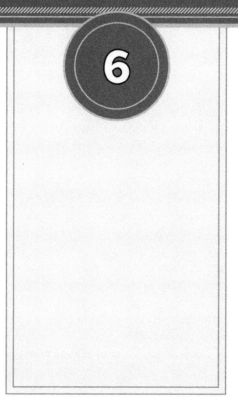

6

Go right now and take a good look at yourself in the mirror. Check your style, head to toe. What do your clothes reveal about you? Believe it or not, what you wear and how you wear it influences the way people see you. At least this is what style guru Nate Retzlaff believes. "Your style is an expression of who you are. Learning to tailor the way you dress to match what you are doing shows people you have style. Inside and out."[1]

Hmm, sounds like Nate has been talking to your parents. He hasn't. Who he does talk with a lot are the most influential clothing brands on the face of the earth. Working as NIKE's design director of Emerging Markets Apparel, Nate Retzlaff's job is to see what the next must-wear look will be, worldwide.

Not only is Nate a style trendsetter, he also knows a bit about what is going through a guy's head when he is getting dressed each morning. "More so today than ever before, guys are able to define who they are by choosing their style. Still, guys need to think about tailoring their clothes to the activity you are doing. Here is an example. I remember my mom harping on me to wear my nice shoes to church or a wedding or something. I felt forced to dress up sometimes. What I now understand is looking nice is about learning how to feel comfortable in a way that is an extension of my personality and still respects the place and people I am around."

According to Nate, the focus of fashion is to express on the outside the man you are on the inside. "Finding your own voice in a way that includes your clothes is a lifelong chase. So be bold. Don't be afraid to make some mistakes. Just learn from your mistakes. When you are choosing a style, my advice is to first be yourself. There are lots of other people out there who look a certain way, the same way. How you dress should be about finding your own voice. Being able to represent your personality through your clothing will make you more confident in your own skin. Second, avoid being inappropriate. Always express yourself in a way that shows integrity and that you really do want to engage with people, even if they are different than you. Learning how to do this is a win-win. Dressing up a little bit or dressing down a little bit without disrespecting the situation is what a man should know about style. The trick is being appropriate without compromising who you are."

Think on Nate's words for a moment and then ask yourself this question: If the world's top apparel brands trust this guy, should I? Now go look in your closet. If you own anything with the globally recognized, trademarked *Swoosh* branded on the side, there is a good chance you already do.

Meet Nate Retzlaff

In addition to working for the Nike "victory" logo, Nate's résumé includes apparel design for a few other companies you may recognize. Do the names Adidas, Dakine, Reebok, X-Games, ESPN, Nissan, Marmot, Salomon, Toyo Tires, or Slingshot sound familiar? Yep, these are the big boys and they have all called on Nate's design genius to promote and advance their brands.

Wash Laundry

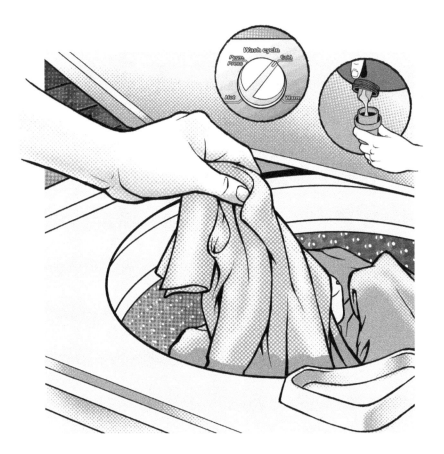

YOU WILL NEED:
- Dirty clothes
- Washing machine
- Laundry detergent

TIME REQUIRED:
- Up to 1 hour

Just because it looks clean doesn't mean it is clean. Clothes get "dirty" when they trap dust, spills, dirt, and sweat in their fibers. On a scale of 1 to Stinky, the kind of "dirty" that sweat produces ranks in at 10+. Your body naturally excretes two types of perspiration. Eccrine is "normal" sweat and is mostly water. Apocrine is stress sweat, a gummy mix of ammonia, carbohydrates, proteins, and fatty acids. The bacteria that live on your skin and in your clothing chow on both sweat types but really prefer your Apocrine buffet. They pay for the free meal by emitting that stanky smell wafting from the clothes pile in the corner of your room. So follow this simple three-step rule and keep it clean: (1) wear it, (2) wash it, and (3) put it away.

STEP 1 **Separate clothes.**

Check labels. Sort clothes of like colors (darks vs. lights) to be washed in separate loads. You may also want to gather socks, underwear, and towels to be washed in a **hot** load.

STEP 2 **Load the washing machine.**

Place one load into the washing machine—darks only, lights only, or a hot wash only.

STEP 3 **Select wash options.**

Set the wash options to match the type of material you are washing. Whites, normal, heavy, and easy care are common settings.

IMPORTANT
The wash option for WHITES usually uses HOT water. Clothes can shrink in hot water, so reset the wash temperature to WARM or COLD if this is a concern.

STEP 4 **Add laundry detergent.**

Read the label on the detergent package. Add the proper measurement to the washing machine. Liquid and powder detergents may need to be added differently, so read packaging instructions carefully.

IMPORTANT
DO NOT use regular detergent in a High Efficiency (HE) washer as it can damage the machine. HE detergent is clearly labeled on the product's packaging.

STEP 5 **Start wash.**

Once clothes, detergent, and any fabric softener have been added, close the washer's door and start the machine.

More Info

There are different types of laundry detergents.

- Powder—Dissolves in wash water. Less expensive than liquid detergents.
- Liquid—Pre-dissolved. Can be used to pre-treat stains on clothes.
- HE liquid—No/low suds required in high efficiency and front load washers.

More, More Info

Fabric Check—Some fabrics shrink in hot water. When exposed to heat, wool and cotton fibers can change shape. This results in shorter sleeves, high-water pants, and that overall one-size-too-small look you'll want to avoid.

Dry Laundry

YOU WILL NEED:

- Clothes from washer
- Dryer
- Dryer sheets

TIME REQUIRED:

- 30 minutes to 1 hour

> Clothes make the man. Naked people have little to no influence in our society.
>
> —Mark Twain

STEP 1 **Clear lint trap.**

Pull and clean the dryer's lint trap to assure proper airflow and dryer efficiency. Lint traps are located close to the cycle option controls or just inside the dryer's door.

STEP 2 **Load dryer.**

Move just-washed clothes from the washing machine into the dryer. Don't let wet clothes sit in the washer, as the scent of mildew will set in and no "Summer Breeze" dryer sheet will fix that.

STEP 3 **Add dryer sheet.**

A dryer sheet softens fabrics and prevents clothes from clinging together from the static electricity produced during tumble-drying.

STEP 4 **Select dry options.**

Set the dryer's options to match the type of fabrics you are drying.

IMPORTANT
The dryer's cycle options include a temperature setting. Clothes can shrink during a hot drying cycle. Adjust the temperature control to a cooler setting if this is a concern.

STEP 5 **Start dryer.**

Once clothes and dryer sheet have been added, close the dryer's door and start the machine.

STEP 6 **Remove clothes.**

Most dryers give you a few minutes of "fluff dry" before they stop tumbling. If you have clothing that you don't want to wrinkle, pull the clothes out of the dryer before the cycle stops and hang or fold them.

Did You Know?

According to FEMA's US Fire Administration National Fire Data Center, there are an estimated 2,900 dryer-related fires in residential buildings each year. Dust, fiber, and lint-clogged dryer vents are the leading cause of ignition. These dryer fires result in an estimated 5 deaths, 100 injuries, and $35 million in property losses annually.

Iron a Shirt

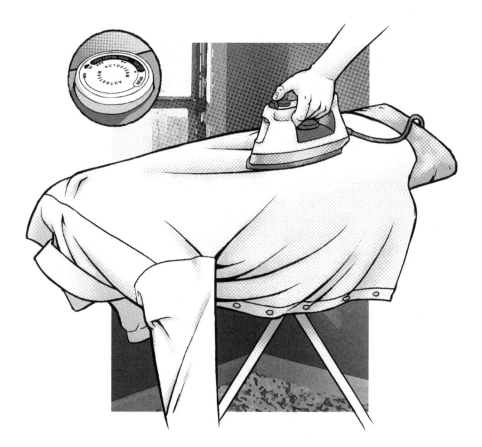

YOU WILL NEED:
- Clean clothes
- Iron
- Ironing board
- Water

TIME REQUIRED:
- 10–15 minutes

Wrinkles are a reality of any man's wardrobe, no matter what you do to prevent them. Even a fresh-out-of-the-dryer shirt may require an ironing to achieve the crisp straight sleeve and crisp collar look you want. Take the time to iron out those wrinkles and people will notice. Don't, and you will be pressed to hear any style compliments that day.

STEP 1 **Open ironing board.**

In a space close to an electrical outlet, open and stand the ironing board.

STEP 2 **Prep iron.**

Add water to steam reservoir, plug iron in, and select the proper fabric temperature setting. (DO NOT overheat the iron, as this can burn and ruin your shirt.) Set iron upright until it is warmed up.

STEP 3 **Iron the collar.**

Smooth the collar top side down on the ironing board. Iron the collar from the edge to the neck seam before flipping to check for smoothness.

STEP 4 **Press the shoulders and yoke of shirt.**

Open the shirt and lay it inside down, flat on the ironing board. Position the shoulders over the narrow side of the ironing board. Iron the fabric from the lower edge of the collar down and across to the top of each sleeve. Move the shirt as needed to reach the full span of the shoulders.

STEP 5 **Press the cuffs.**

With the same approach as taken to iron the collar, press each cuff.

STEP 6 **Smooth the sleeves.**

Lay one sleeve flat on the ironing board with the bottom seam toward you. Press the sleeve with the iron from the top of the sleeve to the cuff. If desired, iron in a crease along the top edge of the sleeve. Turn the shirt and repeat on the other sleeve.

STEP 7 **Flatten the body panels.**

Reposition the shirt so the collar is toward the narrow end of the board. Starting at the top of the shirt, iron down the buttonhole side to the shirttail. Turn the shirt and press the back panel. Turn again to press the button side of the shirt.

STEP 8 **Button and hang.**

Place the shirt on a hanger and button the top button. Hang shirt.

STEP 9 **Clean up.**

Unplug the iron, wait for it to cool, and empty any remaining water from the reservoir. Put the iron and ironing board away.

More Info

If using an unfamiliar or old iron, test first on an old towel or cloth. Mineral deposits will sometimes come out with the steam and ruin your clothing.

Iron Slacks

YOU WILL NEED:
- Slacks
- Iron
- Ironing board
- Water

TIME REQUIRED:
- 10–15 minutes

Walking with pride includes knowing you have the confidence needed to iron yourself a crisp pair of slacks. The look will serve you well when wearing something other than your favorite pair of jeans and will be a skill you need when you want to dress to impress.

STEP 1 **Read the tag.**

Stitched into the waist seam of your slacks is a tag with cleaning instructions. Check these instructions for a proper temperature and steam setting. If steam is required, add water to the iron's reservoir prior to turning it on, and heat it up.

STEP 2 **Lay them down.**

Holding your slacks by the waistband, shake them out a few times to remove any major creases. Make sure the pockets are tucked in properly. Holding the waistband, fold your slacks so one leg is on top of the other. The seams and creases of your slacks should line up.

STEP 3 **Iron one leg at a time.**

After the iron is hot, start at the top of your slacks and slowly run the hot iron over the top leg to eliminate any wrinkles or stray creases. When the top leg is smooth, carefully flip the leg up and repeat with the bottom leg.

STEP 4 **Check the crease.**

Fold the top leg back down into place and check to ensure the creases are in the same place on each pant leg.

STEP 5 **Flip and repeat.**

Turn your slacks over so the recently ironed side is facing down. Repeat STEPS 3 and 4 with the other side of your slacks.

STEP 6 **Turn your iron off.**

Unplug the iron, wait for it to cool, and empty any remaining water from the reservoir. Put the iron and ironing board away.

STEP 7 **Finished.**

If you are not going to wear your slacks immediately, hang or fold them neatly.

Did You Know?

Ironing your slacks is real science at work. The act of pressing the cloth with a hot iron loosens the molecular chains that hold polymer fibers together, stretches them slightly, and causes them to retain their flattened shape as the fabric cools.

Shine Shoes

YOU WILL NEED:

- Towel or newspaper to ensure easy cleanup
- Shoe polish: comes in liquid or wax form
- Horsehair shine brush
- Soft cloth

TIME REQUIRED:

- 30–45 minutes

Many road warrior businessmen jetting through airports stop between flights to get their shoes shined. One of the best shoeshines can be found in the Charlotte international airport. If you are lucky enough to sit in Malik Shabazz's chair, you will get more than small talk while he renews your kicks. In addition to shining your shoes for a few bucks, Mr. Shabazz also offers up some well-polished life advice. Before switching from your right shoe to your left, he may very well tell the man sitting in his chair, "Before people hear you, they see you. The way you look speaks louder about you than your first words do. That's why a good man always has a good shine on his shoes. A good shine tells people that you respect yourself and the way you look when standing next to them."

STEP 1 **Protect the workspace.**

Spread a towel or newspaper on your work surface. Shoe polish can be messy and difficult to remove from fabrics.

STEP 2 **Clean the shoes.**

Use a brush and damp cloth to remove any dirt from the shoes. Be sure to allow shoes to completely dry before applying any shoe polish.

STEP 3 **Apply shoe polish.**

If using liquid polish, glide the polish with the applicator in small circular motions over the entire shoe. If using wax polish, use the cloth applicator that is usually supplied with the polish. The shoe will look cloudy.

STEP 4 **Let shoe dry.**

Wait 15 to 20 minutes to allow shoe polish to dry.

STEP 5 **Get to shining.**

Use the shine brush over the entire shoe. Be sure not to neglect the sides or back of the shoe. Quick, side-to-side strokes ensure maximum shine on your shoes.

STEP 6 **Buff the shoe.**

Using a soft cloth, buff your shoes with a side-to-side motion until your shoes shine. Make sure to buff the sides of your shoes using the same back-and-forth motion to ensure your shoes have a uniform shine.

STEP 7 **Clean up.**

Put all of your shoe shine supplies together for next time and clean up your workspace.

More Info

Every few shines, remove the shoelaces from your shoes. This allows you to get the shoes' tongues clean and polished to match the shine. If you wear stylish colored laces, remove them for each shining and don't re-lace before checking each eyelet for polish residue.

Tie a Tie

YOU WILL NEED:
- Necktie

TIME REQUIRED:
- 2 minutes
  (each)

The tradition of men wearing neckties has survived over 400 years of social and style changes. No longer a fashion statement of class or status, the fabric wedge is as likely to hang in a rock star's wardrobe as a politician's closet. Long and skinny, short and wide, solid, plaid, silk, and synthetic—each look has taken a turn around the necks of men. One necktie truth that has "knot" changed is the fact that a man needs to know how to tie a tie if he ever wants to wear a tie. Here are three different looks and three different ways to tie one on.

The Windsor

Some say King Edward VIII, aka the Duke of Windsor, invented the Windsor knot. Others say the hand of his father, King George V, was the first to loop and tuck the look. Either way the Windsor knot is a wide and especially large knot best suited for a cutaway or wide-collared shirt.

STEP 1

Cross the wide side of your necktie over the narrow side, left to right. The wide end of the tie should hang about 12 inches below the narrow.

STEP 2

Feed the wide end of the tie up through the neck loop.

STEP 3

Direct the wide end down, over, and then back behind the narrow, right to left. The under half of the tie's wide side should now be pointing left and facing out.

STEP 4

Cross the wide side back over the front, left to right.

Pull the wide end back up and through the neck loop.

Guide the wide end down and through the knot. Use both hands to tighten the knot by pulling the narrow end down with your right hand while snugging the knot up to the collar with your left.

The Half-Windsor

STEP 1

Cross the wide side of your necktie over the narrow side, left to right. The wide end of the tie should hang about 12 inches below the narrow.

STEP 2

Tuck the wide end behind and around the narrow side. The under half of the tie's wide side should now be pointing left and facing out.

STEP 3

Bring the wide end up over the neck loop.

Direct the wide end back down and behind the neck loop. The tie's wide underside should now be facing out.

STEP 5

Cross the wide end of the tie back over the front, left to right.

STEP 6

Loop the wide end up, behind, and through the neck loop.

STEP 7

Guide the wide end down and through the knot. Use both hands to tighten the knot by pulling the narrow end down with your right hand while snugging the knot up to the collar with your left.

Four in Hand

STEP 1

Cross the wide side of your necktie over the narrow side, left to right. The wide end of the tie should hang about 12 inches below the narrow.

Tuck the wide end behind the narrow side, right to left. The under half of the tie's wide side should now be facing out.

Cross the wide end of the tie back over the front to the narrow.

Loop the wide end behind, up, and through the neck loop.

Guide the wide end down and through the knot. Use both hands to tighten the knot by pulling the narrow end down with your right hand while snugging the knot up to the collar with your left.

Man Fact or Fiction:
Silk is manly.

Fact. The most popular and highest quality ties are made of silk. To weave a quality silk tie requires approximately 110 silkworm cocoons.

Sew On a Button

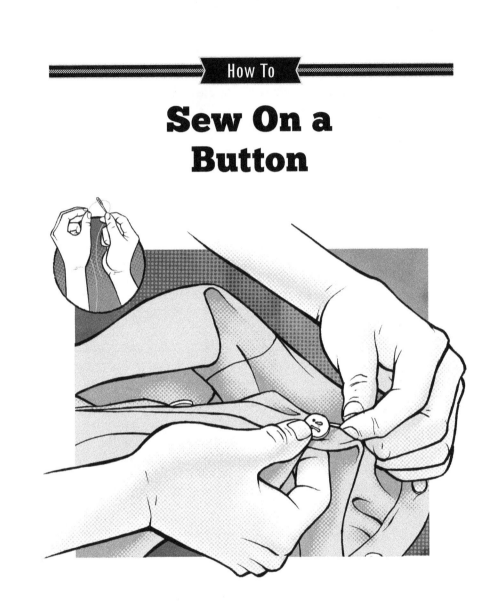

YOU WILL NEED:
- Button
- Thread
- 1 sewing needle
- Scissors

TIME REQUIRED:
- 5–10 minutes

Buttons were originally sewed to clothes as an ornamental fashion statement. It wasn't until the invention of the buttonhole in the thirteenth century that the little round objects gained the functional value we still use today. Traditionally, men's clothing buttons left over right. This was established during the Middle Ages when dueling men needed a fast way to open their coat with the left hand while drawing a sword with the right.

STEP 1 **Thread the needle.**

Push one end of the thread through the eye of the needle. Pull about 12 inches of thread through the eye. Cut the thread off the spool an equal 12 inches from the needle and tie the two ends together in a knot.

STEP 2 **Position the button.**

Place the button in line with other buttons and directly opposite the buttonhole.

STEP 3 **Begin sewing.**

From the underside of the cloth, push the threaded needle up and through the cloth and one of the buttonholes.

STEP 4 **Continue sewing.**

Pull the thread up through the cloth and buttonhole until you reach the knot. Push the threaded needle back down through the opposite buttonhole.

STEP 5 **Continue sewing.**

For buttons with two holes, continue sewing with the needle coming up from underneath the first buttonhole and down through the second. Do this 6 to 8 times until the button is securely in place. If this button has four holes, sew through the buttonholes in a way that creates an X thread pattern on the front of the button.

STEP 6 **Final stitch.**

On the last stitch, push the needle up from the underside of the garment, but not through the buttonhole. Wind the thread around the threads at the base of the button several times to reinforce the shank. Push the needle back down through the fabric. Leaving plenty of thread for the next step, cut the needle free.

STEP 7 **Tie and trim.**

Tie a knot with the two ends of the thread. Once the knot is secure, trim free the excess thread ends with scissors.

Did You Know?

King Francis I of France once wore 13,600 golden buttons on his royal court costume!

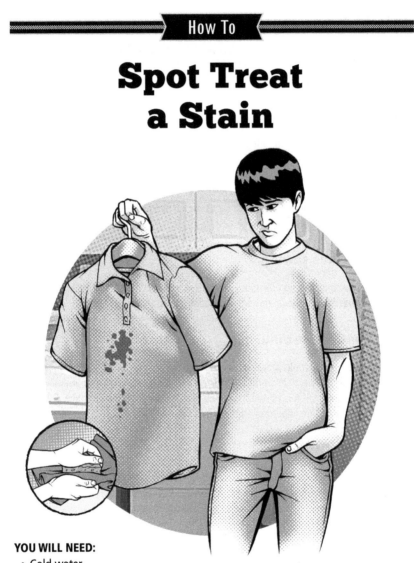

Spot Treat a Stain

YOU WILL NEED:

- Cold water
- Treatment solution—detergent, vinegar, lemon juice
- Paper towel
- Washing machine or professional dry cleaners

TIME REQUIRED:

- 30 minutes

Oops! Your favorite food just took a free-fall dive from your mouth to your shirt. The stain left behind is front and center and setting fast. Don't lose your cool, and whatever you do, don't try to clean it with hot water. Instead, find a clean shirt and take your time to gently work that stain out. Here are some suggestions.

STEP 1 Identify the staining substance.

Different stains require different treatments.

STEP 2 Soak the stain.

Immediately wetting the stain with cold water is a safe start in preventing the stain from setting into the fabric.

STEP 3 Select treatment solution.

Based on the staining substance, pick your treatment. Mild acids like vinegar or lemon juice will fight coffee or tea while laundry or dish detergent work best on grease, blood, chocolate, lipstick, or makeup.

STEP 4 Lightly apply treatment solution.

From the back of the fabric, lightly dab the proper solution to the stain to drive the stain back to the fabric's surface. Do not apply directly down onto the stained area as this may push the stain deeper into the fabric.

STEP 5 Lay stain facedown.

Set the stained fabric facedown on a paper towel. This gives the staining substance something to escape into.

STEP 6 Give it a rest.

Time is your friend, so let the treatment work on the stain. But do not allow the material to dry, as this could set the stain and possibly make it even bigger.

STEP 7 Rinse away.

After 15 to 30 minutes, rinse the stained area under cool water to hopefully wash away both the solution and the stain.

STEP 8 Wash away.

If possible, immediately launder the fabric or take it to a professional dry cleaner.

More Info

Only clean wool fabric using a mild detergent in lukewarm water. DO NOT use bleach. Bleach dissolves wool fabric. Never use hot water! Hot water can cause wool to shrink.

Fold a Shirt

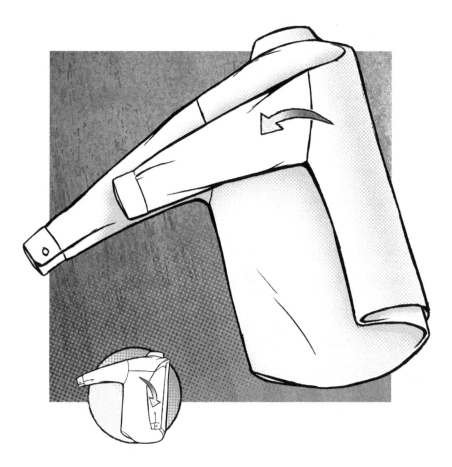

YOU WILL NEED:
- Short- or long-sleeved shirt

TIME REQUIRED:
- 1 minute

No, your floor is not the same as your dresser drawer. Folding your shirts and putting them away will keep each one looking good and smelling fresh. This may seem boring now, but it will save you from the frustrated feeling that comes with digging through a pile of clean clothes only to find your favorite shirts imprinted with a roadmap of wrinkles.

STEP 1 **Button up.**

If the shirt has buttons, button the shirt all the way up.

STEP 2 **Flip it over.**

Lay your shirt facedown on a clean, flat work surface.

STEP 3 **Smooth it out.**

Run your hands across your shirt to smooth all wrinkles or bunches.

STEP 4 **Start on the right.**

Create a vertical fold inward from a point halfway down the shoulder to the bottom of the shirt.

STEP 5 **Fold the sleeve.**

Fold your sleeve forward so that it lines up with the edge of the vertical fold. This will create an angled fold on the shoulder.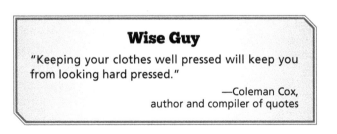

STEP 6 **Repeat.**

Repeat STEPS 4 and 5 with the left side.

STEP 7 **Fold the bottom.**

Take the bottom 6 inches of the shirt and fold it upward.

STEP 8 **Match it up.**

Divide the remaining body of the shirt in half and fold it up to meet the top of the shirt.

STEP 9 **Flip it over.**

Turn the shirt over so that it is facing right side up.

Wise Guy

"Keeping your clothes well pressed will keep you from looking hard pressed."

—Coleman Cox,
author and compiler of quotes

Fold No-Pleat Pants

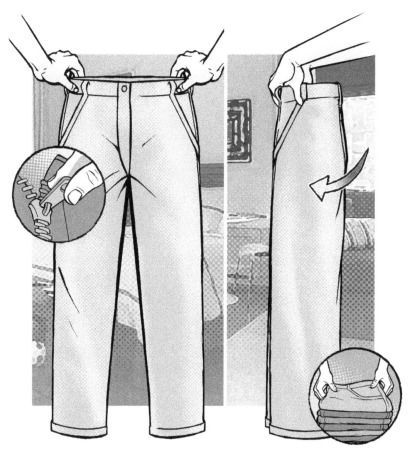

YOU WILL NEED:
- Ironed or wrinkle-free pair of slacks

TIME REQUIRED:
- 10 seconds

Pulled from a pile of clothes, a wrinkled pair of pants looks messy and should never leave the house. Instead, walk tall, knowing that simple tuck-and-stack move you did when folding your clothes kept your pants clean looking, good and ready to be worn out.

STEP 1 **Zip 'em up.**

Start by buttoning and zipping up the slacks.

STEP 2 **Fold in half.**

Hold your slacks on both sides of the waistband with the button and zipper facing you. Fold the slacks in half vertically so the button and zipper make one edge and the waistband's hip seams meet each other.

STEP 3 **Let them hang.**

Hold your folded slacks by the waistband and allow the pant legs to hang.

STEP 4 **Lay them down.**

Lay your folded and lined-up slacks on a flat work surface.

STEP 5 **Fold them again.**

Fold the slacks in half at their midway point, an equal distance between the waistband and ankle cuff.

STEP 6 **One more fold.**

Fold your slacks in half one more time. This fold means that the legs of your slacks are inside the fold.

Did You Know?

Two European immigrants, Jacob Davis and Levi Strauss, started the all-American craze for jeans in 1873. In addition to indigo blue, brown "duck" cotton was sold with rivets on the pockets to increase their strength.

Hang Slacks

YOU WILL NEED:
- Ironed or wrinkle-free pair of slacks
- pants hanger

TIME REQUIRED:
- 30 seconds

Some slacks look their best when properly hung in a closet between wears. So long as they aren't crammed between other hanging clothes, your slacks can stay virtually wrinkle-free and ready to wear anytime, fresh off the hanger.

STEP 1 **Zip 'em up.**

Start by buttoning and zipping up the slacks.

STEP 2 **Let them hang.**

Hold your slacks at the front button and rear seam of the waistband, letting the pant legs hang. The front of the leg crease should run the distance from the top of both legs to the ankle cuffs.

STEP 3 **Fold in half.**

Fold the slacks at their midway point, an equal distance between the waistband and ankle cuff.

STEP 4 **Insert hanger.**

Keeping the ankle cuffs together, slide the hanger up the legs to the midway fold.

STEP 5 **Fold them over.**

Drape your slacks over the hanger at the fold halfway between the waist and ankle cuffs. The waistband and ankle cuffs should meet and be hanging down.

STEP 6 **Hang them up.**

With the slacks hanging neatly, arrange them in the closet so they are not crammed between other clothes.

More Info

When considering purchasing a new pair of slacks, look at the fabric. Patterns like plaids and stripes should match and line up along the front and back seams. All seams, including the waistband, need to be flat and free of ridges, bumps, small rips, or excess material.

SPORTS & RECREATION

7

To be a great man does not mean you have to be a great athlete. In fact, only about .03% of all guys who play organized sports will eventually go pro, and those who do must earn their "man" status the same ways the other 99.97% of guys do. Yet knowing a few basic athletic skills will help any guy gain some respect when he steps onto the field, court, green, or simply into a pickup game at a buddy's backyard barbecue. The secret to athletic performance is not very complicated. Three words, really: Practice makes better.

Still, you dream of going to the pros. Unfortunately the odds are not in your favor. The truth is, more unlucky guys are struck by lightning each year than the number of talented athletes who get drafted into the National Football League each season. Those few exceptional athletes who do make the cut often describe the act of signing their player's contract as a dream come true. But, how long will the dream last? The answer is not what rookies want to hear. The vast majority of professional athletes have surprisingly short careers. Averaging only three years two months, most NFL players are in and out of the league in one-fifth the time they spent preparing to get there. Despite the advantage of world-class training and state-of-the-art body armor, the gridiron is a hazardous jobsite. Competition for starting positions and the ever-present risk of physical injury constantly threaten to end a player's game-time glory.

One NFL player who defied the odds to capture lightning in a bottle is NFL lineman Norm Evans. Standing 6'5" and weighing a solid 250 pounds, the fourteen-year career veteran offensive tackle wore his #73 jersey like an M1 Abrams tank wears camo paint. His commanding combination of speed, agility, and hard-hitting strength made Norm built for battle. Opposing players could do little to escape his explosive power.

Norm Evans's football career spanned terms in both the AFL and NFL. Ten of those bone-jarring years were played with the Miami Dolphins. In his tenure with the team he missed only two games in ten seasons. This commitment to excellence and consistency earned Norm a place in the record books as a member of the NFL's winningest team, the 17–0

Dolphins of 1972. The team captured the NFL's first and only perfect season culminating in a Super Bowl win. Three Super Bowls and two Pro Bowls later, Norm managed to compile 160 starts in 188 games.

So what was the secret to Norm's exceptional performance and unusually long career? He sums up his secret to success in a single word: "Practice." Norm explains:

> Always be practicing the fundamentals. Practice the right thing in the right way and it will become a habit. As a lineman I was constantly practicing the fundamentals. Over and over I worked with coaches who understood the basics of the game. A good coach knows the importance of repetition, of practicing the basic moves time and time again. This was the case for my entire life in football. When I was fourteen years old, I remember the first day I played high school football. You know what we practiced? Running the sweep. Do you know what we did the last day I played football in the NFL? We practiced running the sweep.[1]

Norm's secret is basic and not some get-great-quick scheme. Practice. "It takes true character to understand the time commitment practice requires," he says. Norm is the first to tell you it takes a special kind of athlete to commit their success to repetition. This kind of player must also adopt the mind-set of a student:

> A willingness to practice over and over again means you must be a student humble enough to not think you know everything. You must be willing to learn how to get better, over time. The key ingredient to being a good student is drive. My drive was that I burned to be able to play well. I got this from my dad and his approach to going back and doing something again and again. He would say, "Son, you will never go wrong by doing what is right. If you don't do it right, it's not worth doing." That drive to do well by practicing, by repeating, doing what is right has stuck with me to this day.

Norm also believes there is more to life than football.

> My dad also impressed on me the significance of doing what was right in every aspect of life. He told me to practice things like that I was to respect my mother. And not just my mother, I practiced respecting everybody. This meant I had to be a student and study how to better communicate with people. Communication starts with listening.

My dad's advice is still good today. In every area of life we need repetition. By practicing over a long period of time I've learned how to better communicate with people. It's no different than learning how to do something well, like run the sweep. Mastering the fundamentals takes years and years of practice. Sports, friends, family, faith—never stop practicing and you will never stop getting better.

Meet Norm Evans

Former NFL offensive tackle, fourteen seasons (Houston Oilers, Miami Dolphins, Seattle Seahawks), two Pro Bowls, and three Super Bowls. Norm served as president of Pro Athletes Outreach 1984–2009.

Throw a Football

YOU WILL NEED:
- American football
- Throwing partner

TIME REQUIRED:
- Lots of practice

The dream of all aspiring quarterbacks is to drop back, take aim, and let fly the perfect spiral. NFL pros make the long bomb look effortless, while most average Joes fall short of flinging anything worthy of an instant replay. According to the most accurate arms in the league, passing with precision is a matter of gyroscopic repetition. To consistently thread the needle, you need practice, practice, practice, and then a lot more practice.

STEP 1 **Warm up.**

Get your throwing arm warmed up and stretched out before exercise. This will increase your accuracy and reduce potential injury.

STEP 2 **Get a grip.**

Hold the football toward the back of the laces. Two or three fingers should grip the laces while your thumb wraps around the other side of the ball. Your thumb and index finger should form the letter **L**. Hold the football with your fingertips just enough that your palm is slightly raised off the surface of the ball.

STEP 3 **Assume the position.**

The stance of your feet is important to throwing a football. Move your feet so your body is positioned at a 90-degree angle relative to your target—if you're right-handed, turn to your right, with your left foot forward. Pivot your front foot to point in the direction of your throw and keep your eyes on the potential target.

STEP 4 **Ready your throw.**

Bend your throwing arm into a position that holds the ball comfortably just above your throwing shoulder and below your ear. You can steady the ball with your opposite hand if needed. Now your arm is ready to throw the ball forward in a circular arc.

STEP 5 **Throw the ball.**

In a single motion, drop the ball back a bit behind your shoulder, then move your arm forward in a circular arc while extending your elbow. At the same time, step forward on your front foot and pivot your upper body in the direction of your target. As you release the ball, it should roll off your fingertips, with the index finger last off the ball, which gives it a spiral. Snap your wrist at the release.

This coordinated motion in your arm, body, and feet gives the throw direction and power.

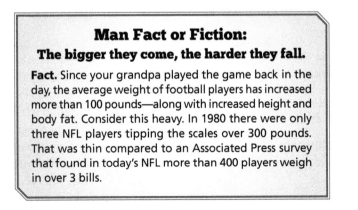

Man Fact or Fiction:
The bigger they come, the harder they fall.

Fact. Since your grandpa played the game back in the day, the average weight of football players has increased more than 100 pounds—along with increased height and body fat. Consider this heavy. In 1980 there were only three NFL players tipping the scales over 300 pounds. That was thin compared to an Associated Press survey that found in today's NFL more than 400 players weigh in over 3 bills.

Shoot a Basketball

YOU WILL NEED:
- Basketball
- Hoop

TIME REQUIRED:
- Lots of practice

Three-time all-American basketball player, two-time inductee into the Basketball Hall of Fame, six-time national coach of the year, and ten-time NCAA Championship winner Coach John Wooden led his teams to a total of 885 career victories. ESPN named Coach Wooden the "best coach of all time," and to this day his undefeated 88-game winning streak stands as the longest in

Division I college basketball history. But what remains the most enduring trait about one of the most revered coaches in the game are the simple inspirational messages he shared with his players.[2]

> "Be more concerned with your character than your reputation, because your character is what you really are, while your reputation is merely what others think you are."
>
> "Be quick, but don't hurry."
>
> "Never mistake activity for achievement."
>
> "What you are as a person is far more important than what you are as a basketball player."

Seldom were Coach Wooden's words directed to hype his players up into giants on the court. Always his inspiration was focused on growing his men to stand tall, be successful, and win in life both in and beyond the game of basketball.

STEP 1 Take a stand.

Balance yourself with your feet shoulder width apart. Face the basket with your dominant foot a half step in front of your other foot. Bend your knees slightly while keeping your back straight and shoulders facing the hoop.

STEP 2 Get a grip.

Spread your fingers and cradle the ball from below in your shooting hand while steadying the ball from the side with your other hand. The basketball should rest on your fingertips, leaving a shallow pocket between the ball and the palm of your hand. Ready the ball for a shot by holding it in the space between your chest and chin.

STEP 3 Take the shot.

Facing the hoop and in a coordinated motion, straighten your knees and jump upward as you raise the ball from the ready position, up in front of your face, while extending your arms upward and forward. Do not bring the ball back to a position near your ear.

STEP 4 Release the ball.

When you reach your full shot extension, release the ball by rolling the shot off the tips of your shooting hand's index and middle fingers. As the ball leaves your hand, snap your wrist so the shot follows an arched path toward the basket. No line drives allowed.

STEP 5 **Follow through.**

Keep your shot form till the ball hits the rim. Don't jump forward or fade backward like some overly confident street ball wannabe. Your feet should land in the same position from where you started the shot.

Did You Know?

Invented in 1891, the game of basketball got its start with players dribbling a soccer ball and shooting it into a peach basket hanging from a balcony.

How To

Kick a Soccer Ball

YOU WILL NEED:
- Soccer ball
- Open space

TIME REQUIRED:
- Lots of practice

The argument rages between Europeans and Americans about what is the proper name of this game. Originally a British gentleman's game called *soccer*, the competitive act of striking a ball forward into a goal has roots dating back through Chinese history to the third century BC. On October 26, 1863, English team officials met to establish a standard set of rules to be played in all matches of the game they termed *football*. Today the most popular team sport played in the world is the "other" football, with the exception of the United States where football ranks #1. American football is different than what the rest of the world calls football, which is known as soccer in the USA. Just like it was termed in 1863 by high-browed Brits in England. There, that should settle the argument. Or not.

STEP 1 **Warm up.**

Get your legs warmed up and stretched out before exercise. This will increase your performance and reduce potential injuries.

STEP 2 **Drop the ball.**

With plenty of space in front of you, drop the ball on the ground.

STEP 3 **Step back.**

Take a few steps back from the ball. You don't need a running start so don't even think about sprinting at the ball from fifteen paces.

STEP 4 **Pick your planter foot.**

Your planter is the foot you'll plant next to the ball while kicking. It's not the one you are going to kick the ball with.

STEP 5 **Approach the ball.**

From two paces back, step toward the ball straight on.

STEP 6 **Place your planter foot.**

When you arrive at the ball, plant your non-kicking foot in a direct line beside the ball. Too far back and you will strike the ball low. Too far forward and you'll strike high.

STEP 7 **Point your planter foot.**

The direction you point your planter foot is the direction you want the kicked ball to travel.

STEP 8 **Swing your leg.**

Bring your kicking leg back to generate some striking speed. In a single motion, rotate your hips and swing your leg forward. Knee straight to pass the ball. Knee bent to shoot.

STEP 9 Strike the ball.

With your ankle locked, strike the ball with your kicking foot. Contact the ball halfway up the laces of your foot for a power kick, or on the inside to direct or pass.

STEP 10 Keep your balance.

Use your arms to balance yourself while kicking. You'll look a bit like a scarecrow at first. So keep practicing.

Wise Guy

"The most important thing in a game of football is to give your all and do things in a responsible way because for sure the victories will come, but there will also be defeats. Anyone who steps onto the playing-field is subject to handle any result."

—Lucimar Ferreira da Silva,
Brazilian pro soccer player

Grip a Two-Seam Fastball

YOU WILL NEED:
- Baseball
- Glove
- Friend to play catcher

TIME REQUIRED:
- Lots of practice

Baseball Hall of Fame inductee Willie Stargell once described the game this way: "They give you a round bat and they throw you a round ball and they tell you to hit it square." Not an easy task, considering many power pitchers can sling a fastball over the plate at nearly 100 miles per hour. But know this: bringing that kind of heat requires strength, accuracy, and lots of practice. Learn to throw a fastball and you will be a hit with more coaches than batters.

STEP 1 **Get a grip.**

The two-seam fastball is gripped with the index and middle fingers laid over the narrow seams of the ball. Position your thumb directly under the ball on the smooth part of the baseball.

STEP 2 **Keep the secret.**

To keep the batter from reading what pitch you are planning, hold and hide the ball in your glove.

STEP 3 **Let 'er fly.**

Hold the ball with your index and middle fingers over the top of the baseball. As you throw, release the ball off your fingertips so it rotates with "backspin."

STEP 4 **Follow through.**

Keep your eyes on the target and allow the follow-through of your throwing arm to cross the front of your body.

Did You Know?

The human body's ability to bring the heat may hit its limit at 100 miles per hour. Why, you ask? The amount of torque required to toss upwards of a buck exceeds the amount of force the elbow ligament can withstand before experiencing damage.

Swing a Golf Club

YOU WILL NEED:
- Golf club
- Golf ball
- Golf tee

TIME REQUIRED:
- Lots of practice

> Golf is the closest game to the game we call life. You get bad breaks from good shots; you get good breaks from bad shots, but you have to play the ball where it lies.
>
> —Bobby Jones

STEP 1 **Get a grip.**

If you're right-handed, grasp the club with your left hand. (Reverse for lefties.) Grip the club with your right hand below your left. Move your right hand's pinky finger to sit between the left hand's index and middle fingers. Your left thumb should set into the palm of your right hand.

STEP 2 **Take a stand.**

Feet shoulder width apart, stand bent forward from the hips with your back in a straight, neutral position.

STEP 3 **Address the ball.**

Stand a comfortable distance from the ball. Close enough that your club's face meets the ball flush, yet far enough back to not crowd your swing. Your arms should be straight.

STEP 4 **Backswing.**

As you swing back, keep your lead forward arm straight yet allow your other arm to bend slightly. Rotate your upper body as you raise your club to create a 90-degree angle between your lead forearm and the club. Your head should remain motionless, looking down at the ball.

STEP 5 **Forward swing.**

Swing your arms down, drawing the club forward in a circular motion. The club's head should lag behind the forearms at 90 degrees yet rapidly unwind to be in near straight alignment with the arms at the point of impact.

STEP 6 **Swing through.**

Past the point of impact with the ball, continue to swing the club around, up, and over your shoulder. A correct swing through will position your body with your belt buckle facing the target, club behind you, and your back foot balanced on its toe.

Man Fact or Fiction:

Shooting a hole in one is a gentleman's call— all a golfer needs to do is keep the ball and have his scorecard signed by the club pro.

Fiction. The fact is, for a hole in one to be "official," the golfer must be playing at least a nine-hole round, play only one ball during the round, and another person must witness the shot.

Putt

YOU WILL NEED:
- Golf club
  (putter)
- Golf ball

TIME REQUIRED:
- Lots of practice

A well-maintained golf green is an absolute work of art. Actually, today's greens are true modern marvels mixed with a bit of "how'd they do that" magic. With the greens hand crafted and machine sculpted, the process of growing millions of blades of grass so short and keeping them perfectly groomed requires knowledge in agronomy, plant pathology, entomology, chemistry, and soil science. Most quality golf courses require their greenskeepers to hold degrees in agricultural or environmental science. Why? Because down below the green-green grass are layers of plastic, pipe, rock, gravel, sand, and even some soil . . . but not much. Add hydroponic watering, fertilizer, chemicals, aerating, sunshine, daily mowing, more chemicals, lots of TLC, and *poof*—you have a perfect putting green. Magic aside, maintaining golf greens properly is no job for amateurs. But anybody can play. Now if only your short game was as good as the grass it's played on.

STEP 1 **Get a grip.**

For righties, grasp the putter with your left hand (reverse the instructions for lefties). Grip the club with your right hand below your left. Move your right hand's pinky finger to sit between your left hand's index and middle fingers. Your left thumb should set into the palm of your right hand.

STEP 2 **Take a stand.**

Feet shoulder width apart, put a little flex in your knees. Draw in your elbows snug to your ribs and tilt your upper body forward. This should allow you to comfortably and gently rest the club's head behind the ball.

STEP 3 **Address the ball.**

Resting the putter just behind the ball, step toward the ball until your toes stand about 2½ putter-head lengths from the near side of the ball. Lean forward slightly and position your body centerline to the ball.

STEP 4 **Make the stroke.**

Ready, aim, stroke. Don't think too hard. Just make a smooth, flowing stroke with the putter toward the cup. One and done.

More Info

An expensive putter can cost upwards of several hundred dollars. A bargain bin putter will put you in the hole only a couple of bucks at your neighborhood yard sale. Neither will make you a better golfer. A keen eye and lots of practice are what pay in the end.

Throw Darts

YOU WILL NEED:
- Set of darts
- Dartboard

TIME REQUIRED:
- Lots of practice

Is this a game of darts or a lesson in mechanical science? A bit of both, actually. Physics controls levers, hinges, joints, acceleration, parabolic curves, deceleration, and your emotions. My emotions? Well, yes, if you get excited about hitting the bull's-eye in a game of darts, you used levers, hinges, joints, acceleration, parabolic curves, and deceleration to strike the very center of the board. Good thing is you needn't have a math addiction to master the game, yet possessing a healthy respect for the laws of physics does help.

STEP 1 **Get a grip.**

Find the dart's center balancing point. Grasp the dart a bit behind the center of gravity with your thumb and your preference of one or two fingers.

STEP 2 **Take aim.**

Think of your eyes, the dart, and the target all needing to line up. Focus on the exact spot on the board you want to hit. This is your target. Don't let anybody walking by distract you. A dart to the head is not a good way to introduce yourself to a girl. (See "How to Talk with a Girl You Like")

STEP 3 **Power up.**

Bend your arm at the elbow and slowly draw your forearm back toward your face. Most accurate throwers stop just shy of the chin or beside the cheek. Avoid direct dart-to-eye contact.

STEP 4 **Accelerate.**

Hinging at the elbow, smoothly accelerate your forearm toward the target. Don't go too fast, you'll lose control. Don't go too slow, you'll lose a toe.

STEP 5 **Release.**

Think naturally. When your arm, wrist, and dart reach the forward-most acceleration point, let the dart fly at the target you haven't taken your eye off of since you got a grip. Raise your elbow and the dart will overshoot the target. Hang on too long and the dart will land too low.

STEP 6 **Follow through.**

Your hand should complete the throw pointing at the target. Not only will this grant you greater accuracy, but you can also point at your shot and proclaim, "Ya man! Did you see that?"

Did You Know?

Due to impairment danger, lawn darts have been banned in the United States since 1988 and in Canada since 1989.

Hit a Cue Ball

YOU WILL NEED:
- Pool table
- Straight pool cue
- Pool balls

TIME REQUIRED:
- Lots of practice

Billiards – General name for cue game sports played on a felt-covered, railed table. The most popular in the world are pool and snooker.

Pool – The family of cue game sports played on a pool table with six rail pockets. One white cue ball is used to strike a combination of up to 15 solid and striped balls into the rail pockets.

Snooker – A cue game sport played on a table that holds six rail pockets and measures 12 ft. × 6 ft. Snooker is played with 22 balls—1 white cue ball, 15 red balls, and 6 additional balls each a different color, including yellow, green, brown, blue, pink, and black.

STEP 1 **Set your bridge.**

Set your hand on the table in front of the cue ball. Slide your thumb up against the side of your index finger into a V shape. This is the bridge and guide for the cue stick.

STEP 2 **Take aim.**

Hold the cue stick at the wide end and set the narrowing end into the V shape of your bridge hand. Keeping the stick level, slowly draw the cue stick back and forth a few times to practice aiming straight at the exact spot on the cue ball you want to strike.

STEP 3 **Practice hit.**

On an open table, practice hitting the cue ball in a straight line from one end of the table, off the opposite cushion, and directly back to you.

STEP 4 **Practice strike.**

Place one billiard ball ahead of the cue ball and practice hitting the cue ball in a straight line into the other billiard ball. Try aiming the cue ball's strike so the billiard ball ricochets off and into a side or corner pocket.

STEP 5 **Play the game.**

With practice and an eye for angles, your game will improve.

Wise Guy

"Never set the pool cue chalk, chalk side down. The blue dust will get all over the rail, your clothes, hands, and you just know that your nose only itches when you have blue fingers."

—Roger Stensland,
billiards player (Jonathan's grandfather)

Pitch Horseshoes

YOU WILL NEED:
- Horseshoe set
- Two 14-inch-tall stakes in the ground, 40 feet apart

TIME REQUIRED:
- Lots of practice

On a dusty field in Bronson, Kansas, Frank Jackson was awarded the first ever World Championship belt for pitching horseshoes. It was the summer of 1910, and at that time no official rules guided players on how to win a ringer. It just so happened that the pits Jackson played on that day resembled the one he had been practicing on back home in Kellerton, Iowa. Four years later in a Kansas City courtroom, a constitution, bylaws, and rules were adopted for playing the game. Doing so changed the sport enough to take it global. Today the game is played in countless backyards, campgrounds, and summer picnics around the world.

STEP 1 **Grip to flip.**

Hold the horseshoe in your pitching hand. There is no rule of how you must grip the 2½-pound horseshoe. The grip that flips the horseshoe when tossed is thumb on top and fingers beneath, slightly off-center of the middle of the shoe.

STEP 2 **Stand behind the foul line.**

To one side of the pit and stake, stand with feet together in preparation to toss.

STEP 3 **Step forward.**

Holding the horseshoe in your pitching hand, extend your pitching arm and swing it underhand and back alongside your body. At the same time, gain balance and throwing rhythm by stepping forward with the leg opposite your throwing arm. So long as your foot does not cross the foul line (which measures 27 or 37 feet from the opposite target stake), step as you please.

STEP 4 **Pitch the shoe.**

As you step forward, underhand swing your pitching arm back and then forward alongside your body. When your pitching arm, hand, and horseshoe all align with your target stake, release or "pitch" the shoe.

STEP 5 **Follow through.**

Let your pitching arm remain raised as the horseshoe flips through the air toward the opposite pit and stake.

Man Fact or Fiction:
Pitching horseshoes is all about power.

Fiction. The fact is, each horseshoe only weighs 2½ pounds. This game is all about aim and strategy.

CARS & DRIVING

8

The days of speeding diecast toys over carpet-paved raceways are behind you. The freedom to drive real horsepower down the open road lies just ahead. Knowing how to safely maintain, operate, buy, sell, and respect a car and its awesomeness is a test of your ability to handle the real thing. The truth is, any guy can drive a car but it takes a true man to handle one. Just such a man is NHRA (National Hot Rod Association) driver, team owner, businessman, family man, and father, Doug Herbert. His experience in cars and heartbreaking personal story of speed is enough to take any driver's breath away.

"The feeling of accelerating from 0 to 100 mph in ¾ of a second and then from 100 to 300+ in the next 3½ seconds is an absolute adrenaline rush," Doug says. As the driver of a supercharged top fuel dragster, Doug Herbert knows the raw feeling of fast and he loves it. "At those speeds it feels like you have been hit by a semitruck. One second you are at a complete stop and then, as quick as you can push down the gas pedal, you're doing more than 100 miles per hour!"[1]

Possessing a rare combination of lightning-fast reflexes, expert driving skills, and the keys to an 8000-horsepower car, Herbert is living the dream. His passion for speed and commitment to hard work have earned Doug the privilege of waking up each day in the fast lane. Yet on January 26, 2008, Doug's dream life turned into a nightmare when he learned that speed, the very thing he thrives on, had claimed the lives of two people he loved—both his sons.

While Doug was preparing to race in the elite NHRA Full Throttle drag series in Arizona, his sons Jon and James prepared to do some un-sanctioned racing of their own back home in North Carolina. A quick trip to the local McDonald's for breakfast was a weekend tradition for the brothers. Nothing was going to stop them from a sausage, egg, and cheese start to the Saturday.

Doug had taught his sons that driving fast was serious business. He had told Jon many times, "Don't drive fast. If you get a ticket, I'll take your car away." But on that rainy morning, the boys forgot their father's warning, ignored the rules of the road, and lost more than the privilege to drive.

Attempting to pass a slower-moving car, the boys failed to see the danger in their choice to speed. In less time than it takes their father to win a race, the boys lost their lives as their car collided head-on with an oncoming vehicle.

In a low tone and with slow words, the father in Doug thinks back. "Nothing could have prepared me for the news. It was like I had forgotten how to breathe. How could this have happened to them? My boys knew that off the track, there was no need for speed, I thought."

Time has passed since the crash, and the racer in Herbert has returned to his dragster. But now as his track speeds exceed 300 mph, he carries the memory, and images, of his sons to the finish line with him. Their faces are proudly pictured on both sides of his dragster, along with this promise: "Forever in our hearts."

Standing next to his race car and beside his sons' images, Doug hopes young drivers will learn from his message for safety. "The one thing I try to share with teens everywhere is that I was sixteen before too, and I should have been dead probably ten times considering all the stuff that I've done. Driving is really dangerous, yet there is a place to go fast. That place is at a racetrack, not running around on the street where people can get hurt." Surely this is the same lesson Jon and James would want all young drivers to learn, and live.

Meet Doug Herbert

Dedicated to saving lives, Doug Herbert has chosen to honor his sons by establishing the B.R.A.K.E.S. Foundation and Driving School for the safety of young drivers everywhere. His hope is that Jon and James's story will help prevent other parents, friends, and families from enduring the pain of losing a loved one in an automobile accident. For more information visit the B.R.A.K.E.S. website at www.putonthebrakes.com.

Shift a Manual Transmission

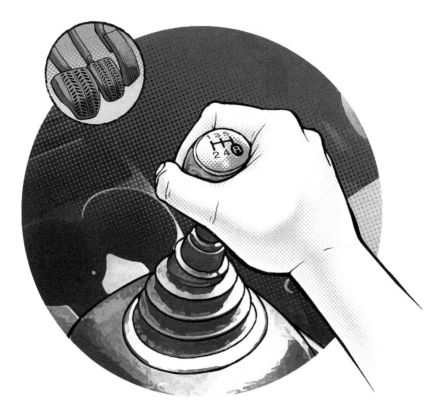

YOU WILL NEED:

- Vehicle with a manually shifting transmission
- Empty parking lot or level road without traffic

TIME REQUIRED:

- 30 minutes plus lots of practice

If you can't find 'em, grind 'em." This gear-shifting advice will get you nowhere fast unless you are planning a trip to the transmission repair shop. Knowing how and when to shift up or gear down is a synchronized act of properly working the pedals and gearshift while steering and even talking to your passengers at the same time. This may seem nearly impossible now, but with practice you will get the hang of it. Till then, do your best not to grind 'em as you find 'em.

STEP 1 **Sit safe.**

Adjust the seat so your body is a comfortable distance from the steering wheel and pedals. Both your knees and elbows should remain slightly bent. The parking brake should be set on. (There is no Park in a manual transmission, so the parking brake is what keeps your car from rolling.)

STEP 2 **Clutch and brake down.**

Notice there are three pedals. From left to right—clutch, brake, and gas (accelerator). With your left foot on the clutch and your right foot on the brake, push both pedals all the way to the floor and hold them there.

STEP 3 **Shift into neutral.**

Use your right hand to move the gearshift into neutral, the center position between the gears where the gearshift will move side to side with ease.

STEP 4 **Start the engine.**

With the clutch and brake still depressed, turn the key to start the car. Release the hand brake.

STEP 5 **Shift into first gear.**

With your right hand, shift the car into "1" (first) gear.

STEP 6 **Release the brake.**

Lift your right foot off the brake pedal and place it on the accelerator (far right pedal).

STEP 7 **Release the clutch while giving it some gas.**

Smoothly lift your left foot, releasing the clutch pedal from the floor. As you release the clutch with your left foot, SLOWLY accelerate. If you release the clutch too quickly, the vehicle will lurch forward and stall. Coordinating the gas and clutch is key to moving forward and will keep the engine from stalling or revving. With practice, you will find the catch point where the clutch engages smoothly.

STEP 8 **Shift up.**

When the RPMs exceed 3,000, shift up to a higher gear. Lift your right foot off the gas, push in the clutch with your left, shift to the next higher gear, lift the clutch, and give it gas again to accelerate.

STEP 9 **Shift down.**

When the RPMs drop below 2,500, shift down to a lower gear. Lift your right foot off the gas, push in the clutch with your left, shift to a lower gear, and lift the clutch.

STEP 10 **Stop.**

As the car slows, shift down one gear at a time and, just prior to stopping, shift into neutral or hold in the clutch pedal to disengage the transmission, braking with your right foot.

More Info

DO NOT over-recline the seat back to look cool. Safely controlling the steering wheel, brake, clutch, and gas pedals is far more important than how you look while driving. Besides, foolish is how you'll look after crashing your car because of a lack of control.

Change a Flat Tire

YOU WILL NEED:
- Spare tire
- Jack
- Lug nut wrench
  (usually incorporated
  into the jack handle)

TIME REQUIRED:
- 15–30 minutes

Spare yourself the roadside embarrassment. Before you get an unexpected flat, figure out where your car's jack and spare tire are located. Practice changing a tire a few times in the safety of your driveway before being forced to actually change a flat on the shoulder of the freeway.

STEP 1 **Remove the spare.**

Pull the spare tire from its storage space in the car. Waiting to remove the spare till after the car is on the jack could be dangerous.

IMPORTANT
When preparing to change a flat tire, always have the car's gearshift lever in Park and set the parking brake. If the car has a manual transmission, shift into 1st gear and set the parking brake.

STEP 2 **Gather your tools.**

Locate and remove from your car the jack and lug nut wrench. (If these are not with the spare, they are probably in a trunk compartment.) Position each beside the car close to where you will be changing the flat tire.

STEP 3 **Loosen the lug nuts.**

Before raising the car, use the flat end of the lug nut wrench to pry free the hubcap (if necessary) and the socket end to loosen the lug nuts. Turn each lug nut counterclockwise until only slightly loose. DO NOT completely remove the lug nuts during this step!

STEP 4 **Position the jack.**

Check your car's owner's manual for the correct place to position the jack under the car.

STEP 5 **Raise the car.**

Jack up the car to a height necessary to both remove the flat tire and install the spare. Remember the spare tire will require more clearance to install than the flat tire requires when removing.

STEP 6 **Remove the lug nuts.**

Finish loosening the lug nuts and place them in a safe location within arm's reach of where you are working.

STEP 7 **Remove the flat.**

Pull the flat tire off and roll it away from your workspace.

STEP 8 **Install the spare tire.**

To ensure proper placement, align the lug holes on the rim with the car's lug bolts and check to be sure the air valve faces out.

STEP 9 **Replace the lug nuts.**

In a crisscross star pattern, work your way around the wheel tightening each lug nut to snug.

STEP 10 **Lower the jack.**

Slowly lower the jack until it's free from the weight of the car.

STEP 11 **Tighten the lug nuts.**

Ensure the lug nuts are fully tightened before cleaning up and driving the car.

Did You Know?

Your car could have a crush on you. NEVER place any part of your body under a car supported by a jack. If the jack gives way, you're stuck. When retrieving an object from under a jacked-up car, use something that extends your reach, like a stick, umbrella, or broom handle.

Jump-Start a Dead Battery

YOU WILL NEED:
- Jumper cables
- Another working battery
  (probably in a buddy's car)

TIME REQUIRED:
- 5–10 minutes

Shocking, isn't it! Somehow your car's dome light was left on overnight and now the battery is drained. No matter how many times you turn the key, there's just not enough juice to get the engine running. To add insult to injury, you're running late! Stop jumping up and down in frustration and try jumping the car's battery instead.

STEP 1 **Find the jumper cables.**

It's always a good idea to carry a pair in the trunk. If yours are "missing," ask to borrow a set.

STEP 2 **Release the hood.**

Pull the hood release lever. It is usually located under the dashboard between the steering wheel and the driver's door.

STEP 3 **Open the hood.**

Reach under the front of the hood to locate the hood latch. Pull it and lift the hood open. If needed, secure it open with the safety arm that either extends up to the hood or down from the hood.

STEP 4 **Position the second vehicle.**

Park the second vehicle next to your car close enough that the jumper cables will reach between the two cars' batteries.

IMPORTANT
Be sure to turn the second car OFF while connecting the jumper cables.

STEP 5 **Connect the red clamps.**

First, connect one red positive (+) clamp to the dead battery's positive (+) terminal. Second, connect the other red positive (+) clamp to the good battery's positive (+) terminal.

IMPORTANT
When connecting the jumper cables, DO NOT touch the positive (+) clamp to the negative (–) clamp or any other metal on either car!

STEP 6 **Connect the black clamps.**

Next, connect one black negative (–) clamp to the good battery's negative (–) terminal. Then connect the other black negative (–) clamp to a metal surface under the disabled car's hood, like the engine block.

STEP 7 **Start your engines.**

First, start the car with the good battery and let it run for a minute or two. Second, with all electrical equipment off (radio, headlights, dome light), try starting the dead battery car. If it doesn't start right away, let the battery charge for a minute before trying again.

STEP 8 **Disconnect cables.**

Once your car has started, immediately disconnect the jumper clamps from both vehicles in reverse order.

STEP 9 **Charge it up.**

Keep your car running for a while before shutting it off to ensure your battery has sufficient charge.

More Info

When disconnecting the jumper cables, DO NOT touch the clamps to each other or any other metal on the car! This can cause the electrical system to short and that's expensive to fix.

Check the Oil

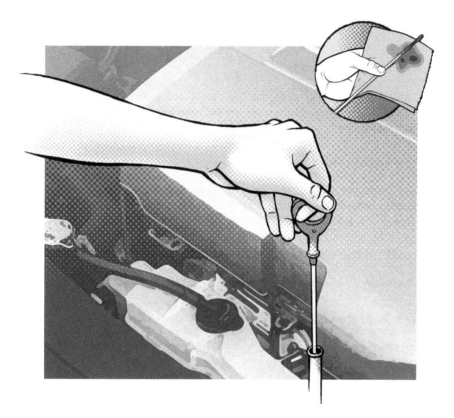

YOU WILL NEED:
- Shop rag or paper towel
- New engine oil
- In some cases, a flashlight

TIME REQUIRED:
- 5 minutes

A dipstick is the measuring device used to check the oil level in a car's engine. A dipstick is also a sarcastic way to describe the guy who forgets to check the oil level in a car's engine. When the car's engine breaks down, the mechanic first checks the dipstick. When he finds the oil level too low, he thinks to himself, *Wow. The driver of this car is a real dipstick for not checking the oil.* Any guy can avoid being a dipstick by learning how to check the oil on the dipstick. Here's how.

IMPORTANT
To get an accurate reading, you will want to check the oil while the car is parked on level ground and while the engine is cool.

STEP 1 **Release the hood.**

Pull the hood release lever. It is usually located under the dashboard between the steering wheel and the driver's door.

STEP 2 **Open the hood.**

Reach under the front of the hood to locate the hood latch. Pull it and lift the hood. If needed, secure it open with the safety arm that either extends up to the hood or down from the hood.

STEP 3 **Locate the dipstick.**

Don't confuse the engine oil dipstick with the one for the transmission fluid. Usually located near the center of the engine compartment, the oil dipstick looks like a long metal loop sticking up out of the engine. It may be a bright color and labeled "Oil."

STEP 4 **Pull the dipstick.**

Pull the dipstick and wipe it clean, using a shop rag or paper towel.

STEP 5 **Replace cleaned dipstick.**

Be sure to press it down all the way. This allows the dipstick to extend fully into the engine's oil pan.

STEP 6 **Pull the dipstick again.**

Hold it horizontally and examine the end to read the oil level. If the oil is above the top line marked "full," the oil level is too high. If the oil is below the bottom line, the oil level is too low. If the oil is between the two lines, the oil level is just right.

STEP 7 **If necessary, add oil.**

Oil should only be added through the hole marked with the words "Engine Oil" on the cap.

STEP 8 **Repeat.**

Follow STEPS 5 to 7 as needed until the oil level is correct.

STEP 9 **Start engine.**

Always replace the dipstick and "Engine Oil" cap before closing the hood or starting the engine.

Did You Know?

If the oil light is illuminated on the dashboard, this means the engine has low oil pressure, not low oil level. Continuing to run the car could severely damage the engine.

Parallel Park

YOU WILL NEED:
- Car
- Parallel parking space
- Patience

TIME REQUIRED:
- 30 seconds

No other low-speed maneuver produces such a high level of pride in a man as parallel parking. To successfully parallel park a car beside the curb on a crowded street is like winning an Indy race. Pedestrians have been known to clap after witnessing an effortless S-shaped parking job. The opposite occurs when people see a guy leave his car "parked" 3 feet from the curb at a

37-degree angle. Don't be that guy. Master the skill of parallel parking and all else is easy driving.

STEP 1 **Find a space.**

On the same side of the street that you are driving on, find a parking space big enough for your car. Put on your right turn signal.

STEP 2 **Line things up.**

Slow to a stop beside the car parked in the space ahead of where you intend to park. A good starting alignment is two to three feet between you and the other car, with the vehicles aligned side-by-side, with the rear bumpers even.

STEP 3 **Check your mirrors.**

Check your side and rearview mirrors for people, obstructions, and other vehicles.

STEP 4 **Check the street.**

Look over your street-side shoulder for traffic. Do not attempt to parallel park while cars try to drive around you.

STEP 5 **Reverse your car.**

Once the middle of your car has cleared the bumper of the parked car, turn the steering wheel all the way right and SLOWLY continue to reverse your car. Check the passenger side and front of your car as you round and pass the bumper of the other vehicle.

STEP 6 **Straighten things out.**

Once your car is at a 45-degree angle to the curb, turn the wheel back to the left. This will direct the nose of your car in behind the other vehicle and bring you into parallel alignment with the parking spot.

STEP 7 **Creep forward.**

Shift into Drive and CREEP your car forward. You may need to steer right to close the gap between you and the curb. Be sure to center your vehicle in the space to leave enough room for the cars in front and behind to exit their spaces.

Man Fact or Fiction:
Men are better parallel parkers than women.

Fiction. The fact is, it doesn't matter if the car is driven by a he or a she. What matters most is the knowledge, practice, and real-world application of mathematic angles, depth perception, and spatial relations. Yep, this is the answer to when you will actually use that boring geometry, and math doesn't care if you are a man or woman.

Back Up a Trailer

YOU WILL NEED:
- Vehicle with trailer in tow
- Friend to spot your direction

TIME REQUIRED:
- 1–5 minutes

Guys with dyslexia are going to love this one. Your reversed way of thinking is about to pay off. Backing up a trailer requires you to think backward. When pushing a payload, turning your wheels right sends your trailer left, while turning left sends your trailer to the right. Think about it, be patient with yourself, and practice as much as you need before attempting to back down the boat ramp. Your pride will thank you, and the post you didn't hit would also thank you, if it could.

STEP 1 **Check the surroundings.**

Walk all the way around the vehicle and trailer. Also walk the route you plan to drive while backing up the trailer. Look for anything you want to avoid running into.

STEP 2 **Straighten out.**

Before driving backward, pull forward far enough to align the vehicle and trailer to be as straight as possible.

STEP 3 **Spot your spotter.**

Have your trusted spotter stand on the vehicle's driver side and toward the rear of the trailer. You must be able to see and hear the spotter at all times.

STEP 4 **Reverse.**

After checking the surroundings and communicating with your spotter, shift the vehicle into "R" (Reverse).

STEP 5 **Slight bend.**

The key to controlling the trailer's reverse direction is to not oversteer. Turn the steering wheel slowly to put a slight bend in the trailer's desired turning direction. Remember, turning the wheel to the right will send the trailer to the left. Turn left and the trailer will head right.

STEP 6 **Follow the trailer.**

Go slow and don't oversteer! If the trailer gets going too far in one direction, stop and pull forward to gain alignment. Check your surroundings, connect with your spotter, and then continue backing up.

STEP 7 **Constantly correct.**

Again, if the trailer gets headed too far in one direction, stop and pull forward to gain alignment. Check your surroundings, connect with your spotter, and then continue backing up.

STEP 8 **Complete the maneuver.**

When the trailer is right where you want it to be, place your vehicle in Park and set the brake. Good job. Your heart rate can return to normal now.

Wise Guy

"When in doubt, get out. Even if you have only 1% doubt of what's behind your vehicle and trailer, stop backing up, get out, and take a look. It's far more embarrassing to hit an unseen post or some guy's fishing boat than to take the time to stop, walk back, spot it, and avoid it."

—Jay Sigafoos,
former driver trainer for UPS

Behave after an Auto Accident

YOU WILL NEED:

- Car
- Another car or ditch, wall, post...

TIME REQUIRED:

- Blink of an eye to crash, 1 hour plus after the crash

Smash 'em and crash 'em. Fun when you are the kid speeding toy cars across hardwood floors into a staged fifty-car pileup. Not fun when you're the man skidding real steel through an intersection into a three-car fender bender. Nobody plans on getting into an accident. That's why we call them "accidents" and not "purposes." Before you overconfidently swerve into the *it-won't-happen-to-me* lane, consider this traffic alert. More drivers between 16 and 24 years old get into car accidents each year than any other age group. In fact, drivers between 16 and 18 years old are the most likely of the most likely to skid into trouble. Why, you ask? Simple. Young, distracted, adrenaline-buzzed guys often accelerate too fast, follow too close, swerve too sharp, or choose to do dumb things with smartphones while driving. But you don't have to be that guy. If you do find your car tangled up with another commuter, here are some important road rules you should follow.

STEP 1 **Stay calm.**

Take a deep breath and remain calm. Immediately following a wreck, your adrenaline will start pumping, so focus on breathing normally to remain calm.

STEP 2 **Check for injuries.**

Check yourself and everybody in your car for physical injuries.

STEP 3 **Stay safe.**

Turn on the car's hazard lights. If possible, move your car to the side of the road, out of the flow of traffic.

STEP 4 **Call 911.**

Even if the crash is minor and the other person is suggesting to "take care of things personally, without cops and insurance companies," always call the police.

STEP 5 **Call your insurance agent.**

Place a call to your insurance agent or insurance company's accident hotline. Explain your situation and listen carefully to their instructions.

STEP 6 **Document everything.**

Take lots of pictures and notes about the accident scene, damage to vehicles or property, and all injuries.

STEP 7 **Exchange information.**

Talk with the other driver and all witnesses. Be sure to exchange important information like names, address, phone numbers, insurance company information and policy numbers, driver license numbers, and license plate numbers. Be polite, stick to the facts, and never say the accident was your fault, even if you think it was.

STEP 8 **Sign nothing.**

Do not sign any document unless it's for the police or YOUR insurance agent.

STEP 9 **Drive safe.**

If the police say your car is drivable, go only as far as needed to get your ride inspected and repaired.

More Info

Never flee from the scene of an accident. Doing so turns your accident into a hit and run. This results in the scene of the accident becoming the scene of the crime.

Behave during a Police Stop

YOU WILL NEED:
- Car
- Lead foot

TIME REQUIRED:
- 10–20 minutes

Blinding red and blue lights strobe through your back window. Your heart skips a beat as small beads of sweat break out on your forehead. Got ya! Settle, you're not busted yet. Now that The Man has your undivided attention, he (or she) wants to have a conversation with you. So pull over, stay calm, and remember there's probably a good reason why the two of you are about to meet. If so, you probably already know what you did. If not, the officer will soon be asking you some questions that will help clarify the reason.

STEP 1 **Pull over.**

Put on your turn signal and look for a safe place to pull to the side of the road. Turn off your engine and wait for the officer to approach your car.

STEP 2 **Stay in the car.**

Keep your seatbelt fastened, turn off the music, roll down the window, and don't even think about reaching for your cell phone.

STEP 3 **Show 'em your hands.**

Rest your hands on the top of the steering wheel so the approaching officer can see them both.

STEP 4 **Provide papers.**

Reach for your license, vehicle registration, and proof of auto insurance only when the officer asks for them.

STEP 5 **Answer truthfully.**

Look the officer in the eyes and be sure to answer their questions truthfully. No lying!

STEP 6 **Accept it.**

You may or may not get a ticket. No matter what the officer decides, accept it like a man. If you want to fight the citation, take your argument to court. Now is not the time, and the side of the road is not the place.

Man Fact or Fiction:
Once an officer pulls you over, they must give you a ticket.

Fiction. The fact is, "the officer will decide on what to do with you once they've had a chance to talk with you. Your truthfulness, attitude, tone of voice, and even your past driving history can influence the officer's decision to ticket or not to ticket."

—Officer B. Harris, Portland Police Department

FOOD & COOKING

9

Dependent guys need somebody else to feed them while an independent man knows his way around the kitchen. Confident enough to cook for himself and certain enough to prepare food for others, a man who can slice, dice, boil, and broil is the meal master everybody likes to be around when it's time for dinner.

Entrepreneur, father, and family man Guy Fieri is one cool cook who knows what it means to make the cut in the kitchen. But long before the spiked-hair, sunglasses-wearing, classic-car-driving celebrity chef appeared on his first food reality TV show, he got his big break by preparing the kind of food people really liked to eat.

Fieri learned to be comfortable in the kitchen when he was young. In an open discussion with fans and reporters at a California food festival, the now famous Guy Fieri recalled cooking his first meal when he was only ten years old. "I remember my dad sitting there. He took a bite of his steak and he looked at me. He set down his fork and knife and I thought, *Oh man, I'm going to get it now.* He looked at me and said, 'You know, this might be the best steak I've ever had.' I just turned into a lion. It was the most amazing feeling in the world."[1] Guy discovered something special about himself that day. "I could cook, make people happy, and my sister has to do the dishes. I'm born to do this," he decided. But like any good man, Guy knew persistence would be the primary ingredient in his recipe for success and the only way he would earn a permanent place at the table in the culinary world.

After cooking his first steak, Guy took another big step up the food chain by learning to prepare and serve one twisted treat. Obsessed with soft pretzels and open to the idea of making money doing what he loved, Fieri built and operated his first pretzel cart when he was in the fifth grade. Sales from the cart he dubbed "The Awesome Pretzel" earned the young businessman enough money to fund the next step in his calling to cook. At sixteen he left the comforts of home to study abroad for eleven months in Chantilly, France. As a foreign exchange student, he gained an appreciation for other languages, cultures, and culinary creations. And this was all in his early days. Guy was just getting started.

It wasn't till after he returned to the States, graduated from high school and college, worked as a restaurant manager, and eventually opened his own eatery that things really began to cook for Fieri. His big break came when he stepped up to the plate and won the Food Network's TV reality cook-off, *The Next Food Network Star*. Viewing audiences not only liked the food he plated, they also liked the way he looked and carried himself, and the level of confidence he possessed both in and out of the kitchen. It was his sense of adventure and willingness to try new things that set Fieri apart. That and his commitment to empowering the next generation of foodies who want to learn how to become independent in the kitchen. Guy's main message for young cooks today is simple. Try, just try. You don't have to be perfect at it. It doesn't mean you are going to do it right now and that it's going to be as easy as a video game to you. But man, nothing makes you feel better than when you make a great meal and the people you eat it with look at it and they go, "Ah!" Ya man, that's real success. Like Chef Fieri, you also have got to be willing to take some chances. You've got to be willing to try. Not everything you make will be perfect. Not anything any chef makes is perfect. But just give cooking a try.

Meet Guy Fieri

Guy Fieri is a celebrity chef, restaurateur, television personality, author, founder of Cooking With Kids (CWK), and proud father of two sons.

Brew Coffee

YOU WILL NEED:
- Coffee brewer
- Ground coffee
- Coffee grinder (if available)
- Coffee filter
- Mug

TIME REQUIRED:
- 15 minutes

Coffee is the original energy drink. From crowned royals to rowdy cowboys, the caffeine bean has pepped people up for centuries. Purchase daily from the local coffee shop and a guy will spill around $1,500 per year on the beverage. Brew at home and the same cup of java will only filter about $300 from the wallet. What a guy does with the extra $1,200 a year is wide open.

Investing in a coffee-bean micro-roaster startup company could prove to be a bold choice.

STEP 1 **Prep brewer.**

Make sure coffee brewer is clean and ready to brew.

STEP 2 **Measure water.**

Add cold water in the brewer's water reservoir to match the number of cups of coffee you want to drink.

STEP 3 **Grind beans.**

(Pre-ground coffee? Skip to STEP 4.) Fresh-ground coffee tastes best. Grind only the amount of beans you need for one brewing.

STEP 4 **Replace filter.**

Put a new coffee filter in the brewer basket.

STEP 5 **Scoop coffee.**

Measure and scoop coffee grounds into coffee filter. Want a light-tasting brew? Use 1 to 1½ tablespoons ground coffee per 6 ounces of water. Bolder taste desired? Use 2 to 2½ tablespoons ground coffee per 6 ounces of water.

STEP 6 **Start brew.**

With the empty coffeepot under the filter, start the brewer.

STEP 7 **Enjoy.**

Once the brewing process is complete, pour and enjoy a cup of hot caffeinated goodness.

More Info

Store coffee beans at room temperature in an airtight, opaque container. To assure a fresh cup of brew, use any bag of beans within one week of opening.

Make Pancakes from Scratch

YOU WILL NEED:
- Ingredients
- Measuring cup
- Measuring spoons
- Large mixing bowl
- Mixing spoon
- Pan or griddle
- Flat spatula
- Cooktop

TIME REQUIRED:
- 15 minutes

Pancakes or Mancakes, it's your choice. Any guy can eat three normal-sized pancakes. Try turning your three flapjacks into one Mancake that hogs the entire plate. Officially Mancakes measure a foot across. Topped with butter, syrup, fruit, or bacon, a double stack of Mancakes often creates its own gravitational pull.

STEP 1 **Gather ingredients.**

This recipe makes eighteen 6″ pancakes or six Mancakes.

3	cups all-purpose flour
3	tablespoons white sugar
3	teaspoons baking powder
1½	teaspoons baking soda
¾	teaspoon salt
3	cups buttermilk
½	cup milk
3	eggs
⅓	cup melted butter

STEP 2 **Mix dry ingredients.**

In a mixing bowl stir together flour, sugar, baking powder, baking soda, and salt.

STEP 3 **Mix in wet ingredients.**

Add the buttermilk, milk, eggs, and melted butter to the dry ingredients.

STEP 4 **Stir ingredients.**

Evenly mix together the wet and dry ingredients until batter is a smooth consistency and free from clumps.

STEP 5 **Let batter sit.**

Allow the batter to sit for five minutes before pouring.

STEP 6 **Preheat pan/griddle.**

Over medium heat, get your cook surface ready. When drops of water sprinkled on the skillet sizzle, it's ready.

STEP 7 Cook pan/Mancake.

Prep the pan with a light coat of butter or cooking oil/spray. Pour a desired amount of batter onto your pan or griddle. When bubbles form and pop on the upside of the cake, flip with the flat spatula to brown the other side.

Wise Guy

"Don't make cheap Mancakes. Always use buttermilk, mix, and then let the batter sit for five minutes before pouring."

—Jonathan

Scramble Eggs

YOU WILL NEED:
- Fresh eggs
- Cooking pan
- Mixing bowl
- Whisk or fork
- Spatula

TIME REQUIRED:
- 5 minutes

Keep it simple. One of the easiest prepackaged breakfasts to cook is an egg. Cracked, whisked, and served with a dash of salt and pepper, eggs make for a protein-rich start to your day. Add a side of toast and glass of juice to make the meal even more nutritious.

STEP 1 **Break eggs.**

Crack open eggs into a mixing bowl. Try two eggs per person for a start.

STEP 2 **Scramble eggs.**

Use a whisk or fork to scramble the egg yolk and white together until they are one solid silky yellow color.

STEP 3 **Heat pan.**

Over medium-high heat, preheat the pan.

STEP 4 **Cook eggs.**

Prep the pan with a light coat of butter or cooking oil/spray. Pour the whisked eggs into the preheated pan. Using the spatula, mix the eggs in the pan until they solidify.

STEP 5 **Enjoy breakfast.**

Transfer the cooked eggs to a plate, add salt and pepper to taste, and eat.

Did You Know?

Eggs have been served for breakfast for thousands of years. East India historians believe chickens were raised to lay eggs from as far back as 3200 BC. Seriously, they weren't yolking around.

Cook Bacon

> Life expectancy would grow by leaps and bounds
> if green vegetables smelled as good as bacon.
>
> —Doug Larson,
> 1924 Olympic gold medalist

YOU WILL NEED:
- Raw bacon
- Frying pan
- Cooking tongs
- Paper towels

TIME REQUIRED:
- 10 minutes

Everything gets better with bacon. Want proof? What is used to make already good food taste better? We add bacon. Like . . . what's better than a burger? A bacon burger. What's better than mac-n-cheese? Mac-n-cheese with bacon bits. Ever had bacon ice cream? You should try it!

STEP 1 **Preheat pan.**

Over medium-high heat, preheat the frying pan. Do not cook bacon on high heat. The bacon will burn and so might your kitchen via a grease fire.

STEP 2 **Add bacon strips.**

Lay each individual bacon strip side by side in the pan.

STEP 3 **Wash hands.**

Always wash your hands after working with raw cuts of meat.

STEP 4 **Flip bacon.**

Using cooking tongs, flip each bacon strip to cook evenly on each side.

STEP 5 **Cook to taste.**

Some like their bacon chewy while some like it crispy. It's your bacon, so it's your choice.

STEP 6 **Drip dry.**

Transfer cooked bacon onto several layers of paper towels. This allows the excess fat drippings to be absorbed by the paper towels.

STEP 7 **Enjoy bacon.**

Once the strips are cooked to your liking, enjoy. Mmm . . . bacon.

More Info

Never pour bacon fat down the sink drain. It will congeal and potentially clog the pipe. Instead, let the drippings cool in the pan and transfer them into a container that can be put in the trash.

Boil Pasta

YOU WILL NEED:
- Large pot
- Colander
- Water
- Pasta
- Salt
- Measuring spoon
- Large spoon
- Stovetop burner

TIME REQUIRED:
- 15 minutes

So you like pasta. What man doesn't? Takeru Kobayashi certainly does. The competitive eater holds a Guinness World Record for slurping up a quarter-pound bowl of spaghetti in only three quarters of a minute. You think you can eat more than that? How about 13,786 pounds of pasta? Chefs at Buca di Beppo Italian Restaurant in Garden Grove, California, served a mighty bowl of the long noodles in a 4,000-gallon pool. Makes sense considering the United States consumes 6 billion pounds of pasta each year. That's an average of 14 pounds per American. Crazy as that may sound, the top pasta spot is held solid by the Italians, who consume an average of 57.3 pounds per person, per year.

STEP 1 **Boil water.**

Fill a large pot about ¾ full with water and bring to a boil. (Add a lid to bring it to a boil faster.)

STEP 2 **Add salt.**

Measure and pour 1 tablespoon of salt into boiling water.

STEP 3 **Measure serving size.**

Most all types of pasta double in size once cooked. So 1 cup uncooked pasta results in 2 cups cooked. A fistful of spaghetti results in dinner for two.

STEP 4 **Add pasta.**

Slowly add pasta to boiling water, no lid needed. Most pasta will cook in 8–12 minutes. Read the package for the recommended cooking time.

STEP 5 **Stir.**

Pasta will stick together if not stirred during the first few minutes of cooking.

STEP 6 **Watch the heat.**

If the water in the pot begins to boil over, turn the burner heat down.

STEP 7 **Test.**

Using a fork, fish a piece from the pot. Once cooled, bite through it. Properly cooked pasta is firm yet tender. This is called **al dente**. The color should be opaque cream all the way through.

STEP 8 **Strain.**

Place a colander in the sink and pour in pot of pasta. Remember the water and steam is hot, so don't get burned. Shake the colander to free any excess water from the pasta. And don't rinse the pasta; the starch that coats it gives it more flavor and helps sauce adhere to it.

> ## More Info
> A colander is a bowl-shaped kitchen utensil with holes in it, used for draining water from food, including pasta.

Make Mashed Potatoes

YOU WILL NEED:
- Potatoes
- Cooking pot
- Colander
- Vegetable peeler
- Knife
- Potato masher or mixer
- Timer
- Butter (2–6 tablespoons)
- Milk (½–¾ cup)
- Salt and pepper to taste

TIME REQUIRED:
- 35–45 minutes

Mashed potatoes are a staple food on the tables of many Europeans, particularly in Ireland and Poland. But did you know potatoes are native to North America? They are. The starchy tuber was not introduced to Europe till 1526. Packed with carbs, the root can be grown year-round in many climates worldwide. Boiled, baked, fried, or smashed, the potato is the side dish of choice by people around the world. If we are keeping score, note this: Americans eat an average of 142 pounds of spuds each year.

STEP 1 **Prepare potatoes.**

Wash and peel the potatoes with the vegetable peeler, digging out the eyes with the end of the peeler.

STEP 2 **Cut potatoes.**

Use a sharp knife to cut each potato into four to six even pieces and put them into a pot. Fill the pot with enough water to fully cover the potatoes.

STEP 3 **Cook the potatoes.**

Bring the water to a boil and then reduce the heat to a simmer. Simmer the potatoes for 15–20 minutes.

STEP 4 **Drain the potatoes.**

When the potatoes are tender enough to be easily pierced with a fork, remove them from the heat and drain them with the colander.

STEP 5 **Add other ingredients.**

Return your potatoes to the original pot. Add milk, butter, salt, and pepper to your preferred taste.

STEP 6 **Start mashing.**

Use a potato masher or mixer to mash the potatoes until they are creamy and free of lumps.

STEP 7 **Serve and enjoy.**

Mmm . . .

Did You Know?

Gardener Peter Glazebrook of Northampton, England, grew a potato of epic proportions. Weighing in at 8 lb. 4 oz., the spud smashed the previous world record of 7 lb. 13 oz.

Oven-Cook Chicken

YOU WILL NEED:

- Chicken
- Baking sheet or roasting pan
- Vegetable oil
- Salt and pepper, to taste
- Basting brush
- Aluminum foil
- Meat thermometer

TIME REQUIRED:

- approximately 1 hour and 30 minutes

Bring the bird indoors. When weather forbids a BBQ, just open the oven and insert a chicken. Prepared right and an oven-baked bird is a great meal to serve to friends, family, or that young lady you want to invite over for a home-cooked meal.

STEP 1 **Prepare the chicken.**

Ensure that the chicken is completely thawed. Remove and discard any giblets from the inner cavity. Rinse the chicken and pat dry with a paper towel. Put your chicken in a baking dish or roasting pan. Brush the chicken with melted butter or oil and season with salt and pepper. Cover the chicken with aluminum foil. Wash your hands to prevent the spread of germs.

STEP 2 **Preheat oven to 400 degrees F.**

Set the oven to 400° and wait for the oven to heat to that temp.

STEP 3 **Cook the bird.**

Put the chicken in the center of the oven and cook for approximately 1 hour. If your chicken is larger than 3.5 pounds, add 10 minutes of cook time per pound. When the chicken has approximately 20 minutes of cook time remaining, remove the aluminum foil to allow the skin of the chicken to brown. Insert a meat thermometer into the thickest part of the chicken thigh. The chicken has finished cooking when the temperature reaches 165° and the juices from the chicken run clear.

STEP 4 **Let rest.**

Once the chicken has reached the appropriate temperature, remove it from the oven and allow it to rest for 10 minutes. This allows the juices to redistribute throughout the chicken.

STEP 5 **Clean up.**

While your chicken is resting, clean the kitchen and wash your hands.

STEP 6 **Carve and serve.**

After your chicken has rested, carve the chicken and serve. Refrigerate any leftovers immediately.

Man Fact or Fiction:
The average chicken nugget is made from quality white meat.

Fiction. The fact is, mechanically separated "pink poultry paste" is what forms most processed chicken nuggets. Fowl parts, including fat, cartilage, organs, and blood, are mixed with artificial additives, molded into bite-sized nibblets, breaded, and served with a side of fries. Thank goodness for dipping sauce . . . right?

Broil Steak

YOU WILL NEED:
- Steak
- Oven
- Broiler pan
- Stove-top skillet
- Olive oil
- Steak seasonings

TIME REQUIRED:
- Cook time 5–15 minutes

No grill! Now what? No problem. Just bring the steak BBQ'n indoors and grill that beef in the oven. Yes, it's possible to cook the perfect cut of meat under the broiler. The consistent temperature control and all-weather access make broiling a steak the perfect alternative to cooking over charcoal.

STEP 1 **Prepare your steak.**

Ensure that your steak is not frozen. Season both sides of your steak and allow it to rest at room temperature for 15 minutes.

STEP 2 **Keep it clean.**

To avoid cross-contamination, never place cooked meat (or poultry or seafood) on a surface that had raw meat on it. And always wash your hands after handling raw meat, especially before handling other food. Same goes for utensils.

STEP 3 **Prepare your oven.**

For electric ovens, adjust the top oven rack so that it is approximately 6 inches from the heating unit. For gas ovens, the broiler is located inside a separate pull-down door, usually below the oven. Turn your oven to "Broil" and put your broiler pan in to preheat it.

STEP 4 **Sear your steak.**

Add 1 teaspoon of olive oil to a skillet on the stove top and turn the burner to high heat. Once the skillet is heated, sear each side of your steak for 60–90 seconds.

STEP 5 **Broil your steak.**

Remove hot broiler pan from your oven and position your steak in the center of the pan. Broil the steak 3–4 minutes on each side for rare, 5–6 minutes each side for medium, and 7–8 minutes each side for well done.

STEP 6 **Let rest and enjoy.**

Remove your steak from the oven and allow it to rest for 5 minutes prior to cutting it. This allows the juices to redistribute into the steak. Your steak is now ready to enjoy.

Did You Know?

Your broiler has two temperature settings: hot and cold. In other words, ON and OFF. If you want to lower the cooking intensity, you will need to lower the oven rack.

Tips for Cooking Meat

How would you like that cooked? When preparing beef or lamb you have choices about how long the meat is over the heat. Some people like their cut blood-rare while others prefer their meal to be mistaken for a charred black hockey puck. Near raw to near petrified, the choices vary as much as people's tastes.

Blue Rare—Barely cooked on the outside, center is cold and very red
Rare—Cooked on the very outside, center is cold and red
Medium Rare—Center is warm and red
Medium—Center is pink and firm
Medium Well—Center has very little pink
Well Done—Center is gray-brown all the way through

Is it done yet? The internal temperature, measured in Fahrenheit, determines the level of cooked or "done" a cut of meat is when fully prepared. The lower the internal temperature, the more rare the meat. The higher the internal temperature, the more thoroughly cooked the meat is when served. Keep in mind that most cuts of meat will still rise by 3°–5° after being removed from the heat source. Always serve pork and poultry at or above their "done" temperatures. Getting sick from undercooked meat is painful and the quickest way to convert to vegetarianism.

Beef

Blue Rare (less than 120°)
Rare (120°–125°)
Medium Rare (125°–135°)
Medium (135°–145°)
Medium Well (145°–155°)
Well Done (155° and above)

Lamb

Rare (135°–140°)
Medium Rare (140°–150°)
Medium (160°–165°)
Medium Well (165° and above)

Poultry

Chicken (165°–175°)
Turkey (165°–175°)

Pork

(150° and above)

Light a Charcoal Grill

YOU WILL NEED:
- BBQ grill
- Charcoal briquettes
- Lighter fluid
- Matches or long-necked lighter

TIME REQUIRED:
- 5 minutes

Grilling—there is something about cooking over an open flame that capitalizes the XY chromosomes in every man. Maybe it's a DNA primal throwback to when our forefathers sat around blazing fires roasting the rewards of a successful hunt. Perhaps it's the fact that BBQ can be smelled from miles away, and to a man, it always smells good. Whatever the reason, the grill master must be respected, and that starts with learning how to stoke charcoal into that perfect amber glow.

STEP 1 **Open vents.**

Open the grill's lower vents.

STEP 2 **Remove top grate.**

Remove the cooking grill.

STEP 3 **Stack the charcoal.**

Create a pyramid shape on the bottom grate by stacking the briquettes 6 inches high by 10 inches across.

STEP 4 **Douse the pyramid with lighter fluid.**

Use an evenly spread douse of about ½ cup of lighter fluid (read manufacturer's specification on the back of the charcoal bag).

STEP 5 **Let lighter fluid absorb.**

Do not ignite the briquettes for 1 full minute after STEP 4. This assures an even flame and avoids the dangers of an explosive flash ignition.

STEP 6 **Ignite the pyramid of briquettes.**

Stand with your face and body turned away from the grill, and ignite the briquettes from the base of the stack. Small flames will move up the pyramid while smoke begins to appear from within.

STEP 7 **Let the briquettes burn undisturbed.**

Within 10–15 minutes the briquettes will be covered with a white/gray ash while the center of the stack glows red-hot.

STEP 8 **Spread the hot briquettes.**

Use a long-handled metal tool to spread the hot briquettes evenly over the bottom grate.

STEP 9 **Replace the cooking grill.**

Allow the cooking grill to heat up prior to placing your food over the heat.

STEP 10 **Grill your food.**

Beef, chicken, pork, fish, and even veggies. It's your choice.

More Info

WARNING! NEVER EVER spray lighter fluid on a lit fire. The flame could travel up the spray-stream and ignite the bottle, causing a serious and life-threatening burn injury.

Grill Steak

YOU WILL NEED:
- Selected cut of steak
- Preheated grill
- Long-handled BBQ utensils, tongs, or fork
- Olive oil
- Steak seasonings

TIME REQUIRED:
- 6–20 minutes

Steak. You don't need to eat at an expensive restaurant to enjoy a great steak. With some basic grill know-how and the right cut of beef, you can earn the reputation of grill master of the best steak on the block.

STEP 1 Remove steaks from fridge.

Around 20 minutes prior to grilling, place steak on a platter, cover, and let sit at room temperature.

STEP 2 Season to taste.

Brush both sides of the steak with olive oil and season with selected spices. An even mix of salt and pepper is a good start.

STEP 3 Sear the outside.

Use BBQ utensils to place the steak over the hottest spot on the grill. For 2–4 minutes sear the steak, one side at a time, until the outside is golden brown to lightly charred. Your seared steak is now officially rare.

STEP 4 Cook the inside.

Move the steak to a cooler space on the grill and cook 3–5 minutes per side = medium rare (internal temp of 135°F), 5–7 minutes = medium (internal temp of 140°F), 7–10 minutes = medium well (150°F).

STEP 5 Enjoy.

Straight from the grill or after letting the cut rest for a few minutes, your steak is ready to eat.

Wise Guy

"There's no need for steak sauce. A good, fresh cut of meat needs only salt and pepper."

—Chris Lyons,
judge with the South Carolina
BBQ Association

Know Your Cuts of Steak

Not all steaks are created equal. Before you head to the butcher's, know what you plan on sinking your teeth into. Learning the names and cuts of meat can be the difference between enjoying a steak that melts in your mouth and suffering through one that chews like leather.

Tenderloin—Also known as a filet or filet mignon, this cut is often considered the "special occasion" steak. Because the area of the cow it comes from doesn't do much work, it remains extremely tender. Cook properly and you will be able to cut this steak with a fork.
Cost—$$$$
Tenderness—Very
Marble—Low
Flavor—Medium

Strip Steak—Also called a New York strip or a Kansas City cut, this meat is perfect for grilling on any occasion. A half-inch of fat usually runs along one side of the steak. Trim this off after grilling so the full flavor of the marbling cooks into the meat.
Cost—$$$
Tenderness—Very
Marble—High
Flavor—Full

Rib Eye—Cut from the center portion of the cow's rib section, the rib eye is a very favorable steak. Cook properly and each juicy bite will seem to melt in your mouth.
Cost—$$$
Tenderness—Very
Marble—High
Flavor—Medium

T-Bone / Porterhouse—This is really two steaks in one. On either side of the T-shaped bone are different types of meat: a strip steak on one side and tenderloin on the other. Keep in mind that the bone affects the way the meat cooks. The portion closer to the bone cooks slower. This means the cut can cook rare to medium at the bone and well to well done on the edges.
Cost—$$$
Tenderness—Very
Marble—Low on the tenderloin side, High on the strip side
Flavor—Medium to Full

Sirloin—Not the best grill steak. This is because sirloin is cut from high on the cow's rear back where the muscle is well used. It's good as stew meat or sliced into cubes and cooked with vegetables on a kabob.

Cost—$$
Tenderness—Low
Marble—Lean
Flavor—Medium

Tri Tip—Seasoned or marinated first, this cut is best cooked at low temperatures over an extended period of time. It is most often served sliced an eighth- to quarter-inch thick and cut across the grain of the meat.

Cost—$$
Tenderness—Low
Marble—Lean
Flavor—Full

Flank—Flank steak comes from a very strong, well-exercised part of the cow's lower abdominal muscle. This makes it a tough meat that is best sliced across the grain when serving. Dry rub seasoning or marinating the meat overnight will help tenderize the cut.

Cost—$
Tenderness—Low
Marble—Lean
Flavor—Medium

Skirt—This cut comes from the plate of the cow. Located below the ribs and in front of the flank, the skirt steak is long, flat, and enjoyed for its flavor, not tenderness. It is best sliced across the grain when serving.

Cost—$
Tenderness—Low
Marble—Lean
Flavor—Full

Grill Pork Chops

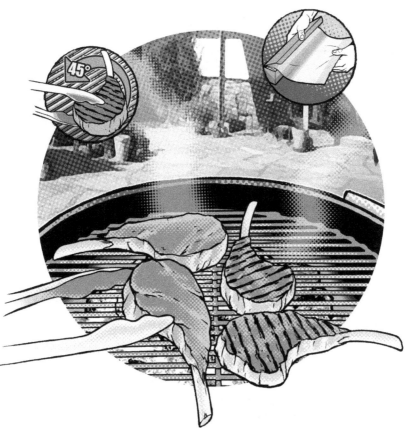

YOU WILL NEED:
- Grill
- Pork chops
- Tongs
- Aluminum foil
- Plate
- Meat thermometer

TIME REQUIRED:
- 20–30 minutes

Pork. Known as "the other white meat," pork is one of the most commonly consumed meats in the world. History holds records of pig farmers dating back to 5000 BC. Tender and flavorful pork chops are good eats any time of the year. Just be mindful of how much you pig out. Savor the swine too much and you'll move to the front of the line for heart disease. Yet pig heart valves have been used to replace damaged human heart valves, so maybe the same pork that ruins a heart can also fix it.

STEP 1 **Fire up the grill.**

Heat your grill to medium/hot. While your grill is preheating, allow pork chops to rest at room temperature to ensure even cooking.

STEP 2 **Place the chops on the grill.**

Using tongs, place the pork chops on the grill and close the lid.

STEP 3 **Rotate 45 degrees.**

For ¾" pork chops, rotate them 45 degrees after 2 minutes. Close the lid for 2 more minutes. For thicker chops, increase time by a couple minutes per side.

STEP 4 **Flip them over.**

Use your tongs to flip over the pork chops. Repeat STEP 3. Total cook time for ¾" chops, 8–9 min. Internal temperature should be at least 150°F.

STEP 5 **Let 'em rest.**

Remove the pork chops from the grill and place them on a plate. Cover them with aluminum foil to rest for 5 minutes before serving.

Did You Know?

The phrase "sweating like a pig" has nothing to do with perspiring pork. Pigs don't sweat, but hot metal does. When pig iron is created from iron ore, the metal is heated to extreme temperatures and then poured into a mold. Until the liquid metal cools, it can't be moved safely. So how does the smelter know when the metal is cool enough to be worked with? When the "pigs" "sweat." As the molten metal cools, the air around it reaches the dew point, causing droplets to form on the metal's surface.

Grill Ribs

YOU WILL NEED:

- Ribs
  (Beef or pork? Beef ribs offer more meat on the bone while pork ribs tend to be more tender)
- BBQ grill
- Plate
- Knife
- BBQ sauce

- Dry rub to season
- Meat thermometer
- Basting brush
- Tongs
- (Optional) Wood chips—mesquite or hickory

TIME REQUIRED:

- Approximately 2 hours

The National Barbecue Association named May the official national BBQ month. No, you are not dreaming; it's true. And to help ignite the summer grilling season, here are some finger-licking facts any man can make a grill-side conversation around.

1. More than a quarter-million moist towelettes are used daily to wipe clean fingers and faces smeared with BBQ sauce.
2. The original barbecue sauce, dating back hundreds of years, consisted of vinegar and pepper.
3. Lyndon B. Johnson, the thirty-sixth president of the United States, hosted the first barbecue at the White House, featuring Texas-style barbecued ribs.

Talk it up, grill it up, and most importantly eat those ribs up. Sweet, sour, saucy, or dry rubbed, the fact remains a rack of ribs on the grill is every meat lover's dream come true.

STEP 1 **Prepare the ribs.**

Cut away excess non-meat tissue and rinse in water. Set the ribs on a plate and massage chosen dry rub seasoning into the meat.

STEP 2 **Let stand.**

Place the seasoned ribs in the refrigerator for one hour.

STEP 3 **Prepare the grill.**

While the ribs season, prep the grill for indirect, medium-heat cooking.

STEP 4 **Grill the ribs.**

Place the ribs on the grill over indirect heat. Cook for 15–20 minutes per side. Remember ribs need to reach 180°F to be fully cooked.

STEP 5 **Brush with sauce.**

Use a basting brush to cover the ribs with barbecue sauce. Leave the ribs over indirect heat for another 10 minutes to infuse the sauce into the meat.

STEP 6 **Remove and serve.**

Once the ribs reach 180°F, they are ready to be cut and enjoyed.

Did You Know?

Adding that smoked flavor to ribs isn't that difficult. First, soak a handful of hickory or mesquite wood chips in water for 10 minutes. Next, drain the chips and place them in a tinfoil tray beside the hot coals. Once the chips start smoldering, you can start to grill the ribs.

Grill a Whole Chicken

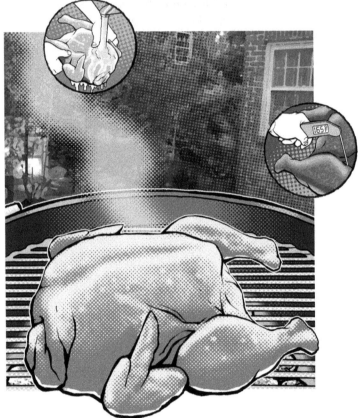

YOU WILL NEED:
- Whole chicken
- Oil
- Salt and pepper, to taste
- Grill
- Tongs
- Meat thermometer

TIME REQUIRED:
- 40–60 minutes

It's odd how people claim so many other meats taste like chicken. When was the last time you heard a guy say his chicken dinner tasted like alligator or rabbit? Never. It's always the other way around. That's because chicken is so popular it has become the "compared to" meal. People forget that chicken really tastes like, well, chicken. And we really like our winner-winner chicken dinners. According to the USDA, each year Americans consume more than 56 pounds of chicken per person—white meat, dark meat, wings, or nuggets. That's a lot of finger-licking good. To make your next chicken meal memorable, forget ordering a processed chicken sandwich and try grilling yourself a whole bird instead.

STEP 1 **Prepare the bird.**

Remove the chicken from the package, rinse, and dry with paper towels.

IMPORTANT
Reach into the chest cavity and remove any "parts" hidden inside. Often butchers stuff the bird's heart, liver, and neck into the cavity for those "waste not, want not" types.

STEP 2 **Prepare the grill.**

Set your grill up for indirect grilling over medium heat.

STEP 3 **Grill the chicken.**

Place the bird on the grill, back side down. Close the lid and grill that bird for 25 minutes.

STEP 4 **Turn the bird.**

Use tongs to flip the bird over onto the breast side. Close the lid and grill for another 20–30 minutes.

STEP 5 **Take its temperature.**

Insert a meat thermometer into the thickest part of the thigh. The chicken is done when any juices run clear and the thermometer reads 165 degrees Fahrenheit.

STEP 6 **Let the bird rest.**

When the chicken reaches the right temperature, remove it from the grill. Let the chicken rest for 5 minutes to allow the juices to redistribute throughout the meat.

STEP 7 **Clean up.**

While your chicken is resting, clean up the grill.

Man Fact or Fiction:
Raw chicken can make you sick as a dog.

Fact. Every year approximately 40,000 cases of salmonellosis (food poisoning) are reported in the US. Raw and undercooked chicken can be infected with salmonella. Symptoms include diarrhea, fever, and abdominal cramps that develop within 12 to 72 hours after infection. Most people recover without treatment.

Grill Fish

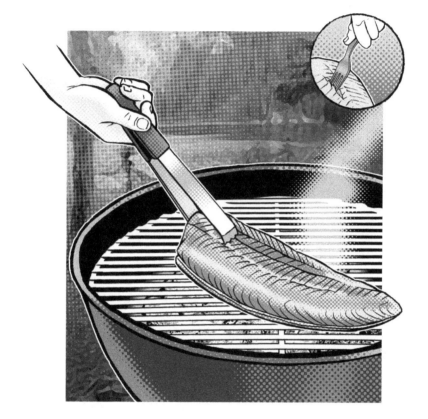

YOU WILL NEED:
- Fish
- Grill
- Knife
- Nonstick spray
- Fork

TIME REQUIRED:
- 15–20 minutes

It's time to grill some gills. Cooked right, and fish over the BBQ is the best. Packed with omega-3 and vitamins such as D and B_2, grilled fish is an easy way to bring a heart-healthy lite-meat balance to your dinner plate. Add a side of rice, fresh veggies, and some fresh fruit and you'll enjoy a healthy meal that can be plated in about 20 minutes.

STEP 1 **Prepare the fish.**

If you are using fresh fish, filet your fish and remove all of the bones. If you are using a filet, make sure your fish is not frozen.

STEP 2 **Prepare the grill.**

If needed (see STEP 3), spray grill with nonstick spray before lighting it. Now heat your grill to medium high.

STEP 3 **Grill fish.**

If you are using fresh fish, place the skin side down on the grill. If you are not using fresh fish, spray the grill with nonstick spray to prevent the fish from sticking.

STEP 4 **Season as desired.**

Sprinkle fresh herbs or desired seasoning on meat side of fish.

STEP 5 **Cook until done.**

After about 8 minutes, use a fork to poke down through to the thickest part of the fish to see if it has cooked all the way through. If it flakes apart and is opaque inside, it is done.

STEP 6 **Remove and serve.**

When the fish has reached 145°F, remove from the grill. Serve immediately.

More Info

Grilling fish with the skin on adds flavor and protects the meat from burning. You can remove the skin after grilling to make serving and eating easier.

Sharpen a Kitchen Knife

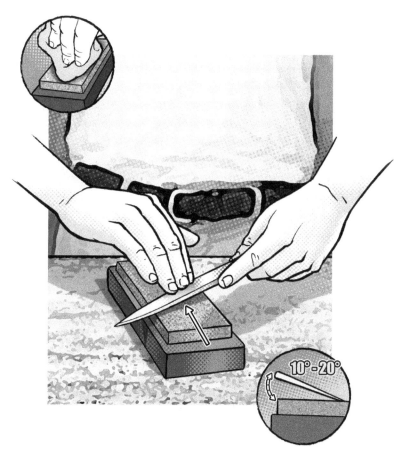

YOU WILL NEED:
- Knife
- Sharpening stone
- Mineral oil

TIME REQUIRED:
- 1–5 minutes

Much can be saved when a knife is kept sharp. A sharp edge saves time, energy, and frustration. It also saves you from experiencing the agony of dull steel not cutting through tough bread yet slicing into your soft finger with ease. Save yourself the pain by carving out a few minutes once a month to carefully sharpen the kitchen knives. Your food will not only look better cleanly sliced and diced, it will taste better knowing no fingers were sacrificed in the meal prep.

STEP 1 **Prepare the stone.**

On the rough side of the sharpening stone, add an ample amount of mineral oil across the entire surface of the stone.

STEP 2 **Angle the blade.**

Hold the knife to the face of the stone at an angle between 10° and 20°.

STEP 3 **Sharpen first side.**

Touch the blade flat on the sharpening stone at the desired angle. Keeping the angle steady, drag the knife—cutting edge first—across the stone while applying moderate pressure. Repeat this 6–12 times per side.

STEP 4 **Sharpen second side.**

Flip the blade to the other side and repeat the sharpening process.

STEP 5 **Repeat with fine stone.**

Flip over the sharpening stone and repeat the process using the fine finish side of the stone. This ensures a smooth cutting edge across the entire surface of the blade.

Wise Guy

"Only a lazy man cuts with a dull knife."

—Roger Stensland
(Jonathan's grandfather)

TOOLS & FIX-IT

10

From professional tradesmen to weekend warriors, men worldwide take pride in the feeling of accomplishment that comes when their "to-do" list becomes their "to-done" list. To get the job done the way it needs to be done, every guy should learn a thing or two about an assortment of tools. With some fix-it know-how, durable equipment, and a craftsman's eye for quality, you too will be equipped with the skills needed to tackle that Do-It-Yourself improvement project.

To assist in making the most of your tool time it's best to learn from the best, and Ned Wolf is just such an expert. Why? you ask. Well, Ned has served for years as the product-training manager of IRWIN Tools, one of the world's leading manufacturers and distributors of hand and power equipment. Every day Ned goes to work in an office/shop/man-dreamland equipped wall-to-wall with the highest quality tools and tool accessories known to man. The grittiest ironworker and the holiest carpenter alike would consider Ned's workspace to be the ultimate work/play space for true craftsmen.

In high demand for his time and expertise, Ned trains the industry's leading workmen yet always looks forward to sharing his talents with guys just starting to build their skills and tool collection. His best tool advice is simple: "Make the work fun."[1]

> When a guy knows about tools, how to use tools, and has a job requiring tools, the work becomes fun. I used to use my tools to play. Now I work with tools and my work has become my play. I've got these tools and I can play with them to get stuff done or even help somebody else get their projects done. If their car needs work, I can play with that. If they have a repair job in their house, well, that's play too. Knowing how to use tools properly converts work into play. It's fun to have fix-it skills. You can make a good impression on somebody you want to impress or even serve others by fixing things out of kindness. Using tools can be about so much more than just getting the job done. Working or playing, fixing or serving, having and knowing how to use tools properly can be both meaningful and fun.

Mr. Wolf doesn't think every guy should fill his garage with the tools and hardware needed to complete any job. But he does believe you will find that building a collection of tools and knowing how to use them will come in handy someday.

Here are fifty items any Do-It-Yourself project man can take pride in owning:

1. Adjustable wrench
2. Broom
3. C-clamps
4. Chalk reel
5. Channellock pliers
6. Chisels
7. Chop saw
8. Circular saw
9. Combination square
10. Crowbar
11. Drill (corded or cordless)
12. Drill bits (for metal & wood)
13. Duct tape
14. Dust mask
15. Dustpan
16. Earplugs
17. Electrical tape
18. Extension cord
19. Flashlight
20. Flathead screwdriver
21. Hammer
22. Hand saws (wood & metal)
23. Hex/Allen key set
24. Jigsaw
25. Ladder
26. Level
27. Needle-nose pliers
28. Open-end/box-end wrenches (standard & metric)
29. Phillips-head screwdriver
30. Pipe wrench
31. Plungers (sink & toilet)
32. Putty knife (1½")
33. Reciprocal saw
34. Safety glasses
35. Sanding block
36. Sandpaper
37. Slip joint pliers
38. Socket set (standard & metric)
39. Speed square
40. Step stool
41. Stud finder
42. Table saw
43. Tape measure
44. Utility knife
45. Utility snips
46. Vise-grips
47. Wire cutters
48. Wire strippers
49. Wood glue
50. Work light

Meet Ned Wolf

Ned Wolf knows tools. He has to, considering he served as the Product Training Manager at IRWIN Tools after building a solid reputation at the Vermont American Tool Group.

Read a Tape Measure

> It's a poor craftsman who blames his tools, while a helpless man has no tools to blame.
>
> —Roger Stensland, carpenter

YOU WILL NEED:
- Retractable tape measure

TIME REQUIRED:
- 5 seconds

Measure twice, cut once. And when the material is expensive, measure three times. This is one of the most valuable lessons every craftsman learns—too often the hard way, after cutting a board too short. Measure up to the task of becoming literate in measurements, and you will save time, money, and the embarrassment of your buddy joking, "So, where do you keep the board-stretching tool?"

STEP 1 **Extend tape measure.**

Pull the end hook to extend the tape measure several feet.

STEP 2 **Lock tape measure.**

Press the automatic rewind switch into the locked position.

STEP 3 **Measuring feet.**

The tape's measurements count up in 1-foot increments from the end hook. Each foot measurement is clearly printed in bold and marked by a line through the tape face.

STEP 4 **Measuring inches.**

Within each foot are inch measurements marked by a solid line through the tape's face.

STEP 5 **Measuring ½ inch.**

Within each inch measurement is a half-inch line.

STEP 6 **Measuring ¼ inch.**

Within each half-inch measurement is a quarter-inch line.

STEP 7 **Measuring ⅛ inch.**

Within each quarter-inch measurement is an eighth-inch line.

STEP 8 **Measuring ¹⁄₁₆ inch.**

Within each eighth-inch measurement is a sixteenth-inch line.

STEP 9 **Retract tape measure.**

Release automatic rewind switch.

More Info

Many tape measures have marks every 16 inches. These indicate the standard distance between wall studs in a home's framing.

Swing a Hammer

YOU WILL NEED:

- Hammer
- Nail
- Board

TIME REQUIRED:

- 3 seconds

> A worker may be the hammer's master, but the hammer still prevails. A tool knows exactly how it is meant to be handled, while the user of the tool can only have an approximate idea.
>
> —Milan Kundera, The Book of Laughter & Forgetting

STEP 1 **Get a grip.**

With a firm grip, hold the hammer toward the end of the handle. Hold the handle tight enough that the hammer will not slip from your grip.

STEP 2 **Take aim.**

Focus on the exact spot you want to strike with the hammer's face. Keep your eyes focused on the head of the nail as you swing the hammer.

STEP 3 **Swing away.**

Lock your wrist and use the strength of your arm and elbow's extension to swing the hammer to directly strike the nail's head.

Tip:
If the nail bends, the face of the hammer is striking the nail's head at an angle. Pull the nail out and start again. The proper strike occurs when the nail's head and hammer's face meet flush, without any angle at the point of contact.

STEP 4 **Drive it home.**

After hitting the nail once, raise the hammer and swing again until the nail is driven to the desired depth.

Did You Know?

There are two types of claw hammers. The curved claw hammer is designed for low impact, finessed nail pulling. The straight claw hammer is made to pry and tear nails free, demo style.

Cut with a Circular Saw

YOU WILL NEED:
- Circular saw
- Lumber to cut
- Measuring tape
- Pencil
- Straight edge
- Cutting surface
- Safety glasses
- Earplugs

TIME REQUIRED:
- 1–3 minutes
  (Depends on a few factors:
  What are you cutting? Is
  the blade of your circular
  saw sharp?)

Brandon Russell, designer, contractor, and former host of TLC's *Trading Spaces* and A&E's *Drill Team*, gives some pointers about using a circular saw:

When cutting with a circular saw, it's important to know something about the saw blade's spinning direction. The type of circular saw used on most job sites for quick framing cuts or to rip boards and plywood spins the blade in a counterclockwise rotation. This means the teeth of the blade are entering the board from below and tearing upward through the wood.

If the good side or face of the wood is up while you cut, the blade may splinter the surface of the board. If you need a smooth cut on the face of the board, flip it over and cut it good side down. Do the math, measure twice, mark your line on the back side of the board, and cut the wood with the good side down. This way the teeth of the blade are ripping into and through rather than through and out of the board.

Keep in mind that the number of teeth on a saw blade plays an important part in the fine finish of a cut. Rule of thumb is the more teeth on a blade, the smoother the cut but the slower the forward speed you should cut. So be patient and go slow.[2]

STEP 1 Mark your cut line.

Measure and mark the line you plan to cut. Use a straight edge and pencil to mark the line you will follow with the guide on the saw.

STEP 2 Prep lumber.

Place the lumber on a surface in a way that the blade of the saw cutting through the bottom of the lumber will not come in contact with any other material.

STEP 3 Put safety first.

Insert earplugs and put on your safety glasses.

STEP 4 Prepare to cut.

Rest the front of the saw (called the shoe) on the material you are about to cut. Make sure the blade is not touching the material. Position the cut guide marked on the shoe to the blade's cut path marked in pencil on the material.

STEP 5 **Cut.**

Pull the trigger on the saw. When the saw blade has reached full speed, start to push the saw away from your body and into the material you are cutting. Follow the cut guide on the shoe and the edge of the blade along the cut path marked in pencil.

STEP 6 **Complete the cut.**

Continue pushing the running saw through the material following the line you drew. As you approach the far side of the board and the end of your cut, make sure you are clear of the piece about to fall to the floor.

STEP 7 **Stop the cut.**

Remove your finger from the trigger in order to stop the saw. Hold the saw in one place while the blade stops spinning. Once the saw has stopped completely, set it aside in a safe location.

Wise Guy

"Always push, never draw a circular saw backwards. The direction the blade is spinning will cause the saw to rapidly lurch back towards you. This could result in you taking an unplanned trip to the emergency room with a nasty cut caused by a runaway saw."

—Eric Longshore,
general contractor, Avon Park, Florida

Use a Drill

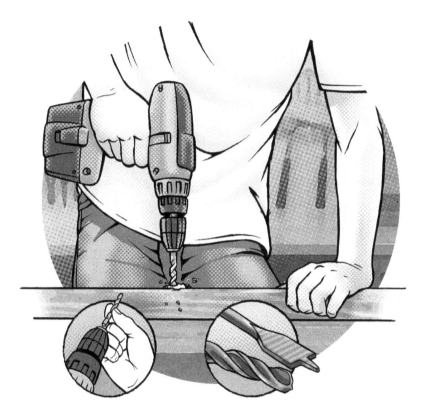

YOU WILL NEED:
- Drill
- Drill bit

TIME REQUIRED:
- 2 to 5 minutes

Arm a craftsman with the right tools and he can drill a hole through about anything. Most weekend warriors need only average home improvement equipment to bore through standard construction materials like wood, metal, and occasionally stone. Extreme drilling demands extreme feats of engineering and requires a really big rig and a bit more power than the average cordless drill. In August 2012 oil engineers set a deep-drilling world record by carving a hole 40,502 feet into the earth's crust. More than 7 miles down, the seemingly bottomless pit is still far from punching through to the other side. That would require a drill capable of withstanding the heat and pressure of the earth's core and a bit about 8,000 miles long. Try stocking that kind of equipment in the average neighborhood hardware store.

STEP 1 **X marks the spot.**

Determine where you wish to drill a hole and mark an **X** in the exact spot.

STEP 2 **Check around.**

Look behind, under, and around the area you want to drill the hole. Ask yourself, "Is there anything behind or under the **X** that my drill bit can damage?" Look for pipes, nails, wiring, the countertop, your hand, or your buddy's hand. And never wear loose clothing or jewelry that could get caught if you lean in too close.

STEP 3 **Select a bit.**

Choose a drill bit appropriate to the material you are drilling through. Different bits are designed for different materials. Check the bit case for the material it is designed to drill through.

STEP 4 **Secure the bit.**

Place the bit into the end of the drill and tighten the keyless chuck. Some older and many large industrial powered drills require securing the bit in place with a chuck key.

STEP 5 **Start the hole.**

Place the tip of the drill bit in contact with your material, apply pressure to the drill, and slowly pull the trigger. Go slow and remember the material you are drilling through determines the proper drill speed. Forcing your way through hard material will dull the bit and can burn the material.

STEP 6 **Reverse directions.**

Once you have successfully drilled through the material, stop the drill. If the bit is stuck in the material, flip the direction switch into reverse. Slowly pull the trigger and reverse the bit back out through the material.

Did You Know?

A drill can also be used as an electric screwdriver. With the proper bit attachment (purchase at any hardware store), you can quickly screw in or reverse out Phillips or flathead screws. Just go slow. With all that power, it is easy to overtorque and even strip your materials.

Did You Also Know?

Water can drill a hole through steel. A wetjet tool directs a high-pressure stream of water at more than 900 miles per hour to cut through metal. Such high-quality H_2O is overpowering when a guy is trying to pressure wash a driveway, yet works great when cutting metal parts in a machine shop.

Use a Crowbar

FULCRUM

YOU WILL NEED:
- Crowbar
- Items that need pulling, prying, or separating

TIME YOU WILL NEED:
- 1–60 seconds

Among the simplest, oldest, and toughest devices in history, the crowbar remains high on the top 10 list of tools every man must own. More than a mindless muscle power tool, a crowbar requires some practiced skill and careful finesse to use properly. Leverage the steel correctly and you will pry your way through difficult jobs with ease.

STEP 1 **Wear gloves.**

No matter what you are doing with the crowbar, you will need to grasp the crowbar firmly.

STEP 2 **Pull nails.**

Use the sharply curved end of the crowbar to pull nails. Hook the head of the nail with the notched end of the tool. Lever the nail out by rolling the tool along the sharp curve.

STEP 3 **Pry apart.**

If you are separating two pieces of wood by prying them apart, use the long end with the flat tip. Insert the end of the crowbar as far between the two pieces as possible. Leverage the crowbar on the slight bend of the chisel tip to separate the two pieces. Continue to push the crowbar into the space you create and repeat the prying motion.

Wise Guy

Shakespeare uses the crowbar numerous times in his writing, including the famous *Romeo and Juliet*. (Act 5, Scene 2, Lines 17–22)

FRIAR LAURENCE

17 Unhappy fortune! by my brotherhood,
18 The letter was not nice but full of charge
19 Of dear import, and the neglecting it
20 May do much danger. Friar John, go hence;
21 Get me an iron crow, and bring it straight
22 Unto my cell.

Use an Adjustable Wrench

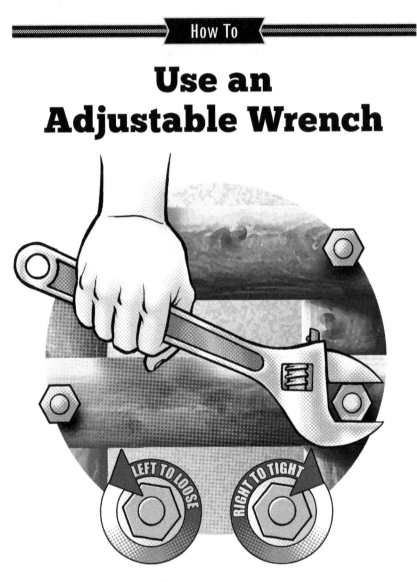

YOU WILL NEED:

- Adjustable (Crescent) wrench
- A bolt or nut in need of turning

TIME REQUIRED:

- 30 seconds to 1 minute

Often referred to as a Crescent wrench, due to the original manufacturer, the adjustable wrench is a staple of every man's toolbox and has been so for over a century. Proper use of an adjustable wrench can save a day, while improper use can end up with the head of a bolt rounded and your knuckles smashed. This condition is also known as a supersized order of frustration with a side of meatloaf knuckles.

STEP 1 **Open jaws.**

Use your thumb and finger to twist open the thumbscrew. This will adjust the jaws of the wrench to the approximate size of the bolt/nut head.

STEP 2 **Position wrench.**

Slide the open jaws of the wrench around the bolt/nut. If the jaws aren't open enough to slide over the head, make another adjustment.

STEP 3 **Tighten the jaws.**

Twist tight the jaws of the wrench until both sides are firmly seated against two sides of the bolt/nut. "Meatloaf knuckles" are caused by the wrench slipping off the bolt/nut and your hand smashing into an adjacent surface. Help prevent meatloaf knuckles by seating the wrench all the way down on the bolt/nut.

STEP 4 **Rotate.**

Rotate the bolt/nut in the direction desired. As silly as it sounds, a good way to remember which way to turn the bolt/nut is "righty tighty, lefty loosey."

Man Fact or Fiction:

Charles Lindberg carried two tools on his record-breaking transatlantic crossing: a screwdriver and a Crescent wrench.

Fact. Due to weight restrictions and the versatility of both tools, he kept his tool selection light and simple.

Use a Level

YOU WILL NEED:
- 3-bubble level

TIME REQUIRED:
- 15 seconds

> I once met a man that framed a house using a defective level ... my guess is he framed the house twice.
>
> —Shawn Sigafoos, general contractor, home inspector

STEP 1 **Pick a bubble.**

Better levels have 3-bubble vials. One is for checking a horizontal grade. One is for checking a vertical grade. The third (not used as often) is set diagonally in the level and used for finding a 45-degree angle.

STEP 2 **Check for *level*.**

Place the tool horizontally (on its side). You want to observe the bubble vial that is also horizontal. If the bubble in the vial is exactly between the two lines, the item can be considered **level**. If the bubble is outside of the lines, adjust your object until the horizontal bubble rests between the lines.

STEP 3 **Check for *plumb*.**

Plumb describes an item standing perfectly straight up and down (vertical). Hold the level against an item vertically and observe the vial sitting horizontally. If the bubble rests exactly between the two lines, the item is considered plumb. If the bubble is not between the two lines, adjust the item accordingly.

STEP 4 **Check for angle.**

The diagonal vial on the level will tell you if an item is at a 45-degree angle. If the bubble is between the two lines when the level is resting on the item, it is close to 45 degrees. If not between the lines, adjust the item until the bubble rests between the lines.

Did You Know?

The bubble level is considered a relatively new tool. The ancient Egyptians built the Great Pyramids to exact specifications using a simple yet highly effective A-frame structure made of 3 pieces of wood and weighted string.

Calculate Square Footage

YOU WILL NEED:

- Tape measure
- Pencil and paper or calculator

TIME REQUIRED:

- Depending on the size of the room(s), probably about 5 minutes

"When will I ever use this class?" you once asked yourself in the middle of a math lesson. Well, today is when. As easy as simple algebra, (L × W = SF), calculating square footage is simple. Get it right and all those math classes just paid off. Get it wrong and you may buy too much material or, even worse, too little.

STEP 1 **Measure the length.**

From one end of the room to the other, measure the room's length.

STEP 2 **Measure the width.**

From one side of the room to the other, measure the room's width.

STEP 3 **Multiply the two.**

Length x Width = Square Footage (L × W = SF).

More Info

If the room is not square, as they rarely are, picture the room as numerous squares and rectangles. For example: An L-shaped room could be broken into one long rectangle and a square. Figure the square footage of the rectangle and then the square footage of the square. Add them together for the total square footage of the room.

Clear a Clogged Sink Drain

YOU WILL NEED:

- Plunger
  (specifically a sink plunger)
- Channellock pliers
  or pipe wrench
- Bucket to catch
  water from drain
- Rags/paper
  towels/old rag
- Cinnamon gum

TIME REQUIRED:

- 5–30 minutes

This is gonna be gross. The degree of gross usually depends on where the sink is located. The kitchen sink will be gross, but clogged food particles are not too bad. Your bathroom sink is going to be grosser. Decomposing hair clogs and toothpaste slime tend to trigger the gag reflex. The public bathroom at work clogged with who knows what . . . that's about as gross as they come. Try to convince your boss to call a plumber.

STEP 1 **Plug sink spill hole.**

Use an old rag to block the sink spill hole. This will keep plunged water from shooting out of the hole.

STEP 2 **Plunge.**

Using a sink plunger, plunge clear the clog. If this fails to drain the sink, continue to STEP 3.

STEP 3 **Locate the P-trap.**

Don't let the name fool you as the P-trap is the section of curved drainpipe shaped like a J. Think of it this way: the P-trap holds just enough water in the pipe to block sewer gases from coming back up through the sink's drain.

STEP 4 **Chew gum.**

Insert a couple of pieces of cinnamon gum into your mouth. Remember the sewer gases mentioned in STEP 3? You're about to smell them, and cinnamon gum might keep you from gagging. Probably not, but it's worth a try.

STEP 5 **Prep space.**

Put a bucket under the P-trap to catch the clogged water and nasty stuff that is about to spill out of the drainpipe.

STEP 6 **Loosen nuts.**

The P-trap has two nuts, one on either side. Since this is designed to be installed by hand, you should be able to loosen these nuts and remove the trap easily. If they are too tight, use the Channellock pliers or pipe wrench.

CAUTION:
Any clogged water is about to spill violently out into the bucket.

STEP 7 **Clear pipes.**

This step can get nasty, but you really must do it. Clear the drain and P-trap of any clogs.

STEP 8 **Replace P-trap.**

When the drain and P-trap are clear, replace the P-trap and tighten the nuts.

STEP 9 **Check for leaks.**

Run water through the drain and make certain the newly cleared pipes do not leak.

Did You Know?

Sink plungers and toilet plungers are designed differently. A sink plunger looks like a ball cut in half with a stick on the end. It has a flat bottom designed to seal over a sink's drain. The toilet plunger includes an extra flange on the open end of the ball. This flange is designed to seal down into and force water through the toilet's drain.

Turn Off a Toilet Water Line

YOU WILL NEED:
- Your hand

TIME REQUIRED:
- 5 seconds

You just used the toilet. After flushing, not everything has gone down the drain. To make matters worse, the water level is rising dangerously close to the top of the bowl. Something bad has happened down in the toilet's pipe, and as you stand there bug-eyed, you realize the situation is about to get worse. Much worse if you don't act fast.

STEP 1 Find the line.

Look underneath the tank of the toilet for a water line. The water line will run from the tank of the toilet to the wall.

STEP 2 Locate shutoff valve.

At the end of the water line running from the toilet to the wall will be a shutoff valve sticking out of the wall. The water line will connect to this valve.

STEP 3 Turn water line off.

Standard shutoff valves work just like the valve attached to your garden hose. Turn the valve clockwise until it no longer turns. At this point the water in the bowl should stop rising. Catastrophe averted.

STEP 4 Read the instructions on "How to Unclog a Toilet."

Man Fact or Fiction:

Yelling "STOP, water, STOP!" will keep a clogged toilet from overflowing.

Fiction. Enough said.

Unclog a Toilet

YOU WILL NEED:

- Plunger
  (specifically a toilet
  plunger)
- Plastic garbage
  bag
- Paper towels

TIME REQUIRED:

- 1–5 minutes

Aclogged toilet can be cause for alarm, particularly if the toilet out of commission is the only one available. Action must to be taken before water spills over the bowl, and though it can be an unpleasant job, the man who fixes the problem is the hero of all waiting outside the bathroom door with full bladders.

STEP 1 **Turn off the water.**

If water in the bowl is getting close to the bowl's rim, turn off the water line behind the toilet. This will stop only the new water from filling the tank and bowl.

STEP 2 **Pick your plunger.**

Make sure the plunger you use is a toilet plunger as opposed to a sink plunger. (See "Did You Know?" in "How to Clear a Clogged Sink Drain")

STEP 3 **Insert the plunger.**

Submerge the plunger into the toilet. If there is water standing in the bowl, this is good; water does not compress and will give you more applied force to the clog than if plunging with only air.

STEP 4 **Plunge.**

Compress the plunger slowly at first. Plunging too vigorously could cause water to fly out of the bowl. For many reasons, you want the water to stay in the bowl.

STEP 5 **Repeat plunging.**

Compress the plunger numerous times before removing the plunger head from the toilet. If the water in the toilet bowl drains freely, you have cleared the clog. If water remains in the bowl, repeat plunging compressions.

STEP 6 **Turn on the water.**

STEP 7 **Clean up.**

Put the plunger into the plastic bag, as people will have a problem with you walking through the house with a dripping toilet plunger. Clean up any spilled water with paper towels.

STEP 8 **Wash your hands.**

Always, always wash your hands after plunging a toilet.

Did You Know?

Long before flushing toilets, chamber pots were used to "relieve" one's self indoors. Once the chamber pot was used, the "contents" were tossed (often out the window).

Check the Circuit Breakers

YOU WILL NEED:
- Flashlight
- Dry hands
- Circuit breaker box

TIME REQUIRED:
- 1–3 minutes

All houses have a circuit box that controls the flow of electricity into and through the home. Usually located in a closet, utility room, or garage space, the circuit breaker box houses multiple individual circuit breakers. Each circuit breaker regulates the "juice" that flows through wires to outlets, switches, and appliances. When too much electricity is drawn down a wire (usually because too many electronic devices are plugged into one circuit), the circuit "flips" or shuts off automatically. This is a good thing, considering the alternative is a literal meltdown and potential fire. Most sane people don't want this to happen. When electricity flows exceed safe limits, the circuit flips off and will require you to manually reset the individual breaker. Don't worry—the process of resetting the flipped circuit and restoring power to your phone charger is simple and safe. Just don't do it with wet hands. Shocking!

STEP 1 **Locate the circuit breaker box.**

Look in the garage, utility room, or closet for a flat metal panel with a metal door.

STEP 2 **Open the door.**

Unlatch the door and open fully.

STEP 3 **Examine circuits.**

Look at the rows of switches. One will be flipped away from the ON position. Rather than flipping fully into the OFF position, it will be halfway between ON and OFF. This is the circuit that needs to be reset.

STEP 4 **Flip to ON.**

Push the switch of the individually flipped circuit all the way off and then back to the ON position. (If the circuit will not stay on there is probably a serious problem. You will need to contact a professional electrician.)

STEP 5 **Close the door.**

Once the circuit has been reset, close the door and enjoy the juice.

Man Fact or Fiction:

Occasionally the electrical contractor takes pride in his work and properly prints labels for the electrical runs on the back of the circuit panel door.
Fact. But don't count on it.

Find a Stud in the Wall

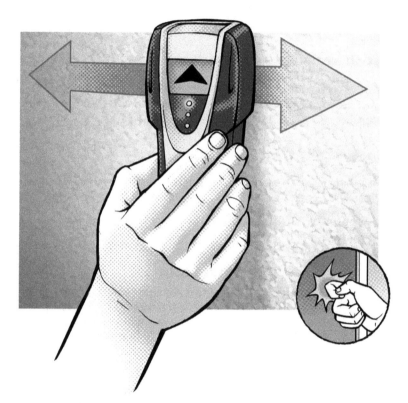

YOU WILL NEED:
- Blank wall
- Electronic stud finder
- Pencil or tape
- Knuckles

TIME REQUIRED:
- 30 seconds

Knock knock.
Who's there?
Stud.
Stud who?
Beep-Beep-Beep-Beep

Ya, um . . . that joke wasn't funny. That's because a stud is a vertical board used in wall framing and not the guy framing the wall. This means a stud finder is never to be used on yourself. The *look, I'm a stud* joke is only funny . . . well, never. Guys who do scan themselves are guaranteed to hear their buddy say, "Nope. False alarm." Men who use a stud finder properly can rest assured the heavy picture they are hanging on the wall stays hanging on the wall.

STEP 1 **Prep the stud finder.**

Turn the stud finder on and set flush against the wall. Activate the detection button on the stud finder to initiate the stud sensor.

STEP 2 **Guesstimate.**

Studs are generally set about 16" apart "on center" (from one stud's center to the next). About where you hope to find a stud, slide the stud finder on the wall in either direction. When the sensor locates a stud, it will alert you with a light, beeping, or both.

STEP 3 **Mark the stud.**

When you have located a stud, mark the approximate center of the stud with a pencil line or tape. Knock on the wall and listen for a solid sound behind the Sheetrock.

More Info

There are two primary types of stud finders: (1) an electronic one that detects differences in the wall's density to identify a wooden beam within the wall; and (2) a magnetic detector that finds metal studs, and some screws or nails in wooden studs.

Hang a Picture

YOU WILL NEED:
- Hammer
- Nail
- Stud finder
- Framed picture

TIME REQUIRED:
- 2 minutes

"It's looking good in here. I just love what you have done with the place. Who is your decorator?" These may not be the exact words you'll hear when your gum-tacked posters come down and framed, hung pictures go up, but you watch, people will notice. Guys who choose to step up the decorating ladder are making two bold statements. First, they know what they like, have a sense of personal style, and are willing to permanently hang said style in a frame. Second, they know how to fix small holes in the wall when they choose to pack up and move. Both are signs of a good man.

STEP 1 **Find the stud.**

Use a stud finder to locate a solid place to hammer in the picture-hanging nail. (See "How to Find a Stud in the Wall")

STEP 2 **Hammer nail.**

Gently and precisely drive a nail into the wall. Leave ¾ of an inch extending out from the wall to hang the picture on. (See "How to Swing a Hammer")

STEP 3 **Hang picture.**

Lower the wire or hanging clasp down onto the nail. Use your visually keen eye or level tool to align the picture to level. (See "How to Use a Level")

Did You Know?

Leonardo Da Vinci's masterpiece **Mona Lisa** is acclaimed to be "the best known, the most visited, the most written about, the most sung about, the most parodied work of art in the world."[3] Painted in the early 1500s, the framed smiling lady has gained great value in the past 500 years. Today she is estimated to be worth approximately $760,000,000.

How to Fix a Small Hole in a Wall

YOU WILL NEED:
- Small can of spackling
- 1½" putty knife
- Medium weight sandpaper

TIME REQUIRED:
- 1 minute prep, 30 minutes dry

Oops. You didn't mean to hit the wall with the edge of your blades, yet now there's a hole that proves your mom was right. Hockey inside isn't a good idea. Lesson learned, the hard way. Good thing the hole is small and fixing it won't be too difficult. Sure it will take a bit longer than netting a goal, but such is the price of indoor sports.

STEP 1 **Prepare hole.**

Carefully remove any chunks of broken drywall.

STEP 2 **Spread spackling.**

Use the end of your finger or putty knife to spread spackling into the small hole. Spread spackling beyond the edge of the hole and so that it rises out farther than the surface of the surrounding wall.

STEP 3 **Let dry.**

Wait until the spackling is fully dry. Some spackling slowly turns from an application color to white, which is an indicator that the product is dry.

STEP 4 **Sand patch.**

Swipe the sandpaper over the dried spackling to knock the texture down to the same level as the surrounding wall.

STEP 5 **Repeat if needed.**

If the spackling dried lower than the surrounding wall, clean the area free of dust, add another layer of spackling, let dry, and re-sand.

STEP 6 **Touchup.**

Paint your patch to match the surrounding wall color.

Man Fact or Fiction:
Toothpaste makes for a quick-fix spackling.

Fact. Yet anything larger than a nail hole is too big to brush up with toothpaste. Man up and fix it right.

Fix a Large Hole in a Wall

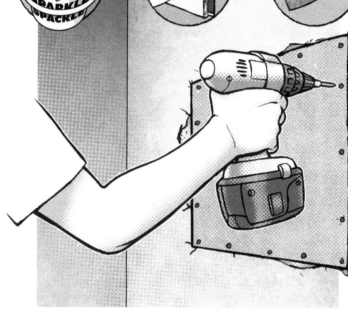

YOU WILL NEED:

- A scrap piece of wood approximately 6" larger than the hole in the wall
- A piece of drywall larger than the hole in the wall
- Drywall mesh tape
- Drywall mud or spackle
- Drywall sanding screen or sanding sponge: rough, medium, and fine
- Drywall screws
- Screwdriver
- Utility knife
- Drywall trowel

TIME REQUIRED:

- 3 hours

So you are goofing around with a buddy inside the house. He pushes you, so you push him back. He pushes you again, and because you're gonna win this one, you push him as hard as you can. He hits the wall and breaks a big hole in the drywall. Busted! No hurt feelings, but you can't say the same about the wall. When your mom gets home, it's going to be a lot easier to show her the damage if you can say, "Don't worry, Mom, I can fix this."

STEP 1 Clean the damaged area.

Remove all loose drywall from the damaged area and then cut the damaged area into a square or rectangular opening.

STEP 2 Insert scrap wood.

Slide the scrap wood into the hole so it spans the opening and secure with drywall screws to either side of the opening. (This wood will be what you secure your drywall patch to.)

STEP 3 Cut drywall patch.

Use a scrap piece of drywall cut to the size of the opening and secure it by screwing the drywall to the wood. Be sure the head of the screw does not break the outermost layer of drywall paper.

STEP 4 Tape the seams.

Lay the mesh drywall tape over the seams. This tape is slightly adhesive and will stick to the drywall.

STEP 5 Apply first coat of mud.

"Bed" the tape with the drywall mud and "feather" the coat of mud 2 to 3 inches beyond the edge of the tape. Don't worry—this doesn't have to be perfectly smooth. Let this coat dry.

STEP 6 Sand first coat of mud.

Using the coarse sanding screen paper, sand the mud enough to knock down the really high spots. Try not to sand into the tape.

STEP 7 Apply second coat of mud.

This time, feather the mud from the center of each strip of tape 4 to 5 inches. Let dry.

STEP 8 Sand second coat.

Use a medium sanding screen to work the dried mud. Look for an edge that is feathered far enough from the patch that you don't see any high spots in the wall. Make sure your sanding doesn't leave new low spots.

STEP 9 Apply final coat of mud.

This should be a very light coat in order to take care of imperfections left in your first two coats. Let dry.

STEP 10 Sand third coat.

Use very light pressure with your fine sanding screen. Don't sand too hard or you'll need a fourth coat. This should leave your patch ready for primer and paint.

Wise Guy

"I'm two decisions away from putting up drywall for a living—I am, and there's nothing wrong with that, but whatever I got, it's through the grace of God, and I've got to use it right."

—Jeff Foxworthy,
American comedian

How to
Talk Like a Man
100 Terms Men Need to Know

Lower your voice and listen up. Men have their own language and it's time for you to learn a few basic words. Know them and you will begin to hear them. Use them correctly and you will be welcomed into a higher level of manliness. No grunting or chest pounding required.

ampere Often called an *amp*, an ampere is a unit of electric current named after the French mathematician and physicist, André-Marie Ampère.

arc The curved contour of an item like a bow. Also the shape and name of an electrical discharge as current jumps the gap between two electrodes, including your finger and a bare wire.

auger A corkscrew-shaped hole-drilling device.

axe The long-handled, metal-head-bladed tool used by skilled woodsmen to fell or split lumber. Not to be confused with trendy body wash and cologne products.

bed A layer of drywall mud, clean place you sleep at night, dirt-filled plot where gardens are planted, or the enclosed back of a small truck.

bit You have options: a small measurement or portion, sharp drilling tool, metal mouthpiece for a horse, or the basic unit of information in digital communications.

bow A ship's forward hull or the respectful action of bending forward at the waist during a formal introduction.

braise Cooking method used for less-tender meats. The meat is browned slowly and thoroughly on all sides, after which a small amount of liquid is added to the pan. The pan is covered and the meat is simmered over very low heat until tender.

chuck Could be the name of a guy you know or just the clamp that holds a drill bit in place. Not to be confused with the action of throwing or throwing up.

clutch The pedal or lever that engages or disengages gears while shifting a car. Also the feeling you get when you learn to shift without grinding the gears. *Yes! Started my car on a hill and didn't even grind the gears. That was clutch.*

cord Flexible electrical wire that fits into a wall socket, a measure of rope, or a stacked quantity of wood measuring 4' x 4' x 8' with a volume of 128 cubic feet.

corporate The combined group of people who function with one culture driven by shared rights, privileges, and liabilities. You know, like a business.

creditor The person or organization loaning out money to a debtor.

cubic zirconia A colorless form of zirconia that is very similar to diamond in refractivity and appearance, aka a fake diamond.

damper An adjustable plate in a chimney or stove for controlling the draft. Also the feeling you get when you forget to open the damper before lighting the fire. *The smoke filled room really put a damper on the party as everybody coughed and wheezed.*

debtor The person or organization owing money to the creditor.

dipstick The measuring device used to check the oil level in a car's engine. Also the sarcastic term mechanics use to describe the guy who forgets to check the oil level in his car's engine.

dovetail The tail of a dove . . . or the fan-shaped interlocking joint that fits together two pieces of wood.

D.T.R. Abbreviation for *Define The Relationship*. The conversation a couple has to determine if they are officially "going out," "dating"—you know, boyfriend and girlfriend.

earnings Salary or wages.

empathy Understanding and being aware of and sensitive to the feelings, thoughts, and experience of others even though you have not experienced or are not experiencing the same.

equity The quality of being just or fair. Also the actual value of property after subtracting any loans or liabilities.

ethos The disposition, character, and values of a person, group, culture, or movement. Best described as "who we are."

feather Bird clothes. Also, and more practical to men, to *feather* is to apply a thin tapering layer or coating of a spreadable substance like drywall mud or cake frosting. WARNING: Don't lick drywall tools clean.

fee A fixed charge for a professional service.

flashing Sheet metal for reinforcing or weatherproofing joints and angles on a roof.

fuse A safety device containing wire that melts and breaks a circuit if the electrical current exceeds reliable levels.

galvanized Steel coating that contains a thin layer of zinc to prevent corrosion. Often applied to garbage cans, fencing, nails, and other metal pieces that will be exposed to moisture.

gratuity A favor or gift given in return for services. Most often given in the form of money. Also called a *tip*.

grill The action of cooking food over an open flame. The front of a car, truck, or metal set of teeth. To question another person with great intensity.

grout A thin layer of plaster or mortar used to finish or to fill cracks.

hatchet A small, short-handled axe intended to be held and used in one hand.

head The cranium supported atop your body's shoulders, which seats your ability to reason. The toilet supported below a ship's deck, which seats your ability to relieve yourself.

helm The steering mechanism of a ship. Also the location from where the ship's captain directs the vessel's course.

hitch The attachment extending from the rear of a vehicle to which you join and tow a trailer.

ID vs. id Your ID is an officially issued identification card imprinted with your photograph and the unique features of your life. Your id is the most basic part of your personality that identifies and unconsciously seeks to meet basic life needs.

inboard Housed within the craft, vehicle, or vessel.

in debt The owing of money, goods, or services to another person or organization.

indirect heat Method of heating or cooking food to the side of the heat source.

jack A device used to lift heavy objects. The face card below a queen. The name of a guy you know.

Jane Doe The generic female name of a person who is unknown or needs to remain anonymous.

jib The forward-most triangle-shaped sail on a sailboat. The long arm of a construction or loading crane.

John Doe The generic male name of a person who is unknown or needs to remain anonymous.

joist Any parallel beam located in and supporting the floor or ceiling.

keel The centerline structure along a boat's hull.

kilt A traditional knee-length, pleated cloth garment worn by men of the Scottish Highlands.

kingpin Large main bolt holding other structural units together. Pull it and everything else comes loose.

labor Hard physical labor. Like unloading a 8½-ton delivery of jagged rocks or delivering a pudgy 8 lb. 6 oz. baby. Lucky you're a man—unloading the rocks is much easier than pushing a baby out of your body.

lever A pivoting bar used to help move heavy objects.

lowbrow Low intellectual context or culture.

mentor An experienced and trusted advisor who tells you what you need to hear and not just what you want to hear.

moorage The place and fee for storing a boat or aircraft.

mortgage The charge of property, by a debtor to a creditor, for the value of the property to be paid back in a set contractual period of time.

mulligan When a player, often a golf buddy with a bad slice, gets a second chance to perform a move or action. Also referred to as a *do-over*.

National Guard Brave men and women serving in a branch of the military partially maintained by each state but also available to be deployed by the federal government.

nest egg Money saved for long-term future use.

Nike The mythological Greek winged goddess of victory and one cool brand of athletic performance equipment.

Nobel Prize A coveted international prize given each year for outstanding work in one of six categories; physics, chemistry, medicine, economics, literature, and the promotion of peace.

oath A promise regarding your future actions or behavior.

octane rating standard performance measure of motor fuel. The higher the octane number, the higher level of compression the fuel will withstand before igniting.

open-minded The willingness to consider new ideas without prejudging.

Outback The remote inland region of Australia.

pasteurized The process of heat-treating food products to the point of partial sterilization. It has nothing to do with church.

pension A payment made from an investment fund to the retired person who contributed to the fund during their working career.

pickup A small truck with an enclosed bed. To collect and put away your stuff. A weak attempt to introduce yourself to a girl you like.

port A harbor-side city or town. The left side of a boat, indicated with a red navigation light.

quart The measurement of liquid equal to a quarter of a gallon.

quest A long and honorable search for something valuable, like your manhood.

question An expression worded to gain information. Ask great questions and you will get great information. Ask weak questions and you will get weak information. Ask no questions and you will get no information. So ask great questions.

rappel Lowering yourself down a near vertical surface using a rope to control your descent.

rent The payment made to a land or vehicle owner for use of their property. *Rent*: A long-running New York Broadway rock musical about a group of young "starving artists" and musicians struggling to "make it" in New York City's Lower East Side.

resign Voluntarily leaving a job.

rip To use force to tear, pull, or separate material.

rudder A hinged vertical piece used to steer a boat from the stern.

sear To use intense heat to burn or scorch the surface of something, like a juicy steak, pork roast, or leg of lamb.

slack The loose or unused part of a rope. A lazy worker, hence making them a nonworker.

sorry To feel sympathy toward a person or situation. An authentic apology you should offer when you have been exposed as acting in a pitiful way.

spotter A person who keeps an eye on the situation to maintain safety.

starboard The right side of a boat, indicated with a green navigation light.

stern The rear or back section of a boat.

stud The vertical board within a framed wall that supports the vertical load of a structure. Usually 2" x 4" or 2" x 6" wooden boards, studs are most often spaced 16 inches apart. Nailing into wall studs is a solid way to secure a picture frame, shelving, or bracket needed to display your vintage guitar. Also a male breeding animal valued for the quality of his genetics.

tab An open unpaid bill for products or services already delivered.

taxes Required payment to a governing body from the income or profits of an individual or business.

tension The emotional state of feeling like you are paying too many taxes. The physical state of being pulled tight or stretched out.

tenure The permanent status granted for a person's job or position.

transom A small window over a door or larger window.

U-bolt A bolt shaped like the letter *U* that is threaded on both ends. Go figure.

undercarriage The supporting structural framework under a vehicle.

universal joint A mechanical joint that transfers power though a shaft over a range of angles. Also called a *U-joint*.

valor Great courage in situations of great danger.

vise A stationary tool with movable jaws used to hold objects in place while being worked on. Usually attached to a solid surface like a workbench or truck bumper.

volt The international standard measurement of potential electronic force. Voltage is the variable that determines the severity of a shock should electricity pass through a conduit, like your body. For example, hold the ends of a 1.5-volt AA battery and you won't feel a thing. Touch the connections of a 120-volt wall socket and you will jump in pain from the shock. Get tased by the 50,000-volt pulse of a police stun gun and you are on the ground, incapacitated, and probably soiling yourself.

well-groomed The appearance of a clean, neat, well-dressed man.

whetstone A fine-grained stone used to sharpen metal-edged knives and tools.

winch A low-geared crank or motor-driven lifting tool that winds rope, cable, or chain around a drum to lift or lower heavy items.

XY chromosome The thread-like molecules that carry DNA hereditary information specific to the gender of male.

yoke A crosspiece that unites separate pulling forces to become one.

youth hostel Cheap sleeping accommodations for urban backpacking tourists or travelers.

zed The pronunciation of the letter *Z* by Canadians and other British-influenced English speakers.

Zodiac Small inflatable boat.

Notes

Part 1 Women & Dating

1. Quotes in this introduction are from Les Parrott, interview by author, December 2012.

Part 2 Social Skills & Manners

1. Quotes in this introduction are from George Toles, interview by author, February 2013.

Part 3 Work & Ethics

1. Cory Cotton, interview with author, January 2017.
2. Cory Cotton, *Go Big* (Carol Stream, IL: Tyndale, 2011), 4.
3. Cotton, interview with author.
4. Cotton, *Go Big*, 108.
5. Cotton, interview with author.
6. Cotton, *Go Big*, 169.

Part 4 Wealth & Money Management

1. www.daveramsey.com/company/about-dave.
2. Dave Ramsey, *The Total Money Makeover Workbook* (Nashville: Thomas Nelson, 2003).
3. Dave Ramsey and Sharon Ramsey, *Financial Peace Revisited* (New York: Viking Penguin, 2003), 5.
4. Ibid., 20.
5. Dave Ramsey, *Total Money Makeover: Classic Edition: A Proven Plan for Financial Fitness* (Nashville: Nelson Books, 2013), 5.
6. Mandi Woodruff, "Financial Guru Dave Ramsey Tells Us Why He Cuts Up Credit Cards on Air," BusinessInsider.com, April 23, 2012, http://www.businessinsider.com/dave-ramsey-hates-credit-cards-2012-4.
7. Chris Carpenter, "The Total Money Makeover: An Interview with Dave Ramsey," CBN.com, http://www.cbn.com/family/familyadvice/carpenter-daveramseymoneymakeover.aspx.
8. http://www.daveramsey.com/article/our-favorite-dave-quotes-of-2009/lifeandmoney_other/.
9. Copyrighted phrase coined by Dave Ramsey.
10. Dave Ramsey, "A Weird View of Money," LifeChurch.tv, http://www.youtube.com/watch?v=Af1zc0qhr8o.

11. John Maxwell, quoted by Dave Ramsey, *Total Money Makeover*, 59.

12. Dave Ramsey, *CBS Morning Show* interview, February 10, 2009.

13. Samuel Fleichacker, *On Adam Smith's* Wealth of Nations: *A Philosophical Companion* (Princeton, NJ: Princeton University Press, 2004), 68.

Part 5 Grooming & Personal Hygiene

1. Quotes in this introduction are from Thomas Frieden, interview by Bill Phillips, editor-in-chief of *Men's Health* magazine, on a Google+ chat, June 13, 2013.

Part 6 Clothes & Style

1. Quotes in this introduction are from Nate Retzlaff, interview by author, February 2013.

Part 7 Sports & Recreation

1. Quotes in this introduction are from Norm Evans, interview by author, November 2012.

2. "The Wizard's Wisdom: 'Woodenisms,'" ESPN.com, June 4, 2010, http://sports.espn.go.com/ncb/news/story?id=5249709.

Part 8 Cars & Driving

1. Quotes in this introduction are from Doug Herbert, interview by author, September 2009.

Part 9 Food & Cooking

1. Quotes in this introduction are from Guy Fieri's appearance at Disney's California Food and Wine Festival, 2010.

Part 10 Tools & Fix-It

1. Quotes in this introduction are from Ned Wolf, interview by author, September 2009.

2. Brandon Russell, interviewed by author, September 2013.

3. John Lichfield, "The Moving of the *Mona Lisa*," *The Independent*, April 2, 2005.

Jonathan Catherman is a leading education consultant and trainer specializing in the character and leadership development of youth. An award-winning cultural strategist, Jonathan speaks worldwide about the principles and strengths that empower greatness in children, teens, and young adults. The father of two sons, he sees daily the importance guys place on gaining respect and avoiding embarrassment. As both a parent and a professional, Jonathan is committed to assisting young men in the making to experience success and significance as they mature into manhood and lifelong leadership. Jonathan, his bride, and their boys live in Huntersville, North Carolina. Learn more at www.jonathancatherman.com.

> If I had my time over, I would do the same again. So would any man who dares call himself a man.
>
> —Nelson Mandela

CPSIA information can be obtained
at www.ICGtesting.com
Printed in the USA
LVHW010840291118
598485LV00018B/467